National poetry Anthology 2009

This anthology features winning
entries from an annual competition
which is free to enter. Winners receive
a free copy of the anthology and vote
for one overall winner who receives
£1,000 cash and a magnificent trophy
to keep for life. If you would like to
enter for next year's anthology, send a
loose second class stamp and up to
three poems (20 lines and 160 words
maximum each), to United Press,
Admail 3735, London, EC1B 1JB by
the annual closing date of June 30th.
You can also call us on 0870 240
6190 or visit our website on
www.unitedpress.co.uk

LADY IN RED

He glanced at the picture that hung by a string,
Then looked again at the lady within,
So aloof, yet alone, so silent, withdrawn,
An impression so gentle, yet sad and forlorn.
In misty surroundings she walked through the wood,
He longed to be with her, if only he could.

Alone and lonely, walked the lady in red
With a scarlet umbrella to cover her head,
Lovely and lonely like a painting of old,
A picture to hang in a frame made of gold.
A picture of dreams, so vague yet so deep,
Does she laugh? Does she cry? Does she sigh?
Does she weep?

His chair is now empty, he's gone from the place
Where he gazed at the lady dressed in crimson and lace,
But glance at the picture and then look once again,
Look past the umbrella that's shielding the rain,
Look through the mist, just past her head
And you may see him waiting for the lady in red.

Roy Lewis, Merthyr Tydfil, Wales

A poem has earned Roy Lewis £1,000 and a national title.

Roy (73) of Merthyr Tydfil, has won the £1,000 first prize in the biggest annual free to enter national poetry competition there has ever been.

"Roy's prizewinning poem is evocative and eerie," said United Press Managing Director Peter Quinn, who made the presentation. "It is a beautifully crafted piece of gothic poetry in the mold of Edgar Allan Poe. It's a really worthy winner in a competition which has grown bigger every year and culminated in this - the best and biggest National Poetry Anthology we have ever produced. There are almost 300 winning poems in it this year and the standard is better than ever."

Roy received the cash prize of £1,000 plus a magnificent trophy to keep for life in a presentation at Merthyr Tydfil library. He is the first ever Welsh winner of the prize.

"I love to write poetry because it expresses things that I can't say in everyday words," explained Roy.

"I saw a poster for the competition and even though I've been writing poems for 50 years and not submitted anything, I realised that it was a great new opportunity. The competition was free to enter and had a big cash prize. When I saw the poster I told myself - *I can do that. I might as well try, because I've got nothing to lose.* It was a real shock when I got the news that I'd won. To be voted for by almost 300 other poets is a very humbling experience. I'm absolutely stunned."

Many thousands of poems were entered for this UK-wide annual competition which began in 1998, aimed at unearthing new poetry talent.

Out of all the entries which are submitted every year over 250 are picked to represent different regions in the UK and all are printed in the annual National Poetry Anthology. Each author receives a free copy of the book and votes for the best poem in it.

Many of the poets in this latest edition have given press interviews and read their poetry on air. Some have appeared together on BBC radio to read their winning poems.

PREVIOUS
NATIONAL POETRY ANTHOLOGY
WINNERS

2000 Louise Rider, Amersham, Buckinghamshire
2001 Ann Marsden, Saltburn, Cleveland
2002 Pamela James, Weston Favell, Northamptonshire
2003 Christine Masson, Sevenoaks, Kent
2004 Eileen Hudson, Rochdale, Greater Manchester
2005 Lawrette Williams, Drayton, Somerset
2006 Peter Button, Lancaster, Lancashire
2007 Stephen Holden, Preston, Lancashire
2008 Roy Lewis, Merthyr Tydfil, Wales

Foreword

Time has passed with amazing speed. I find it hard to believe that it's now ten years since the publication of the first National Poetry Anthology. In those ten years this annual publication has grown to become a major part of the United Kingdom's poetry landscape.

This book is the result of the biggest free-to-enter annual poetry competition there has ever been. Every year we receive many thousands of entries from poets young and old, new and established. Every year we pick over 250 regional winners from right across the UK - including Scotland, Northern Ireland and Wales. Every winner receives a free copy of the book and votes for their favourite poem. The winner of this vote receives £1,000 in cash.

Every year we never cease to be amazed by the wonderful quality of work submitted to us. It's truly amazing that many of these poets have never had anything published before. We at United Press are immensely proud of the fact that we have helped so many thousands of poets to be acknowledged and appreciated as published writers.

There is no other annual competition which has given anything like as much help to budding poets. It's our aim that the anthology keeps on growing every year and keeps on unearthing great poetry.

Peter Quinn, Editor

Contents

Each poet listed in this contents of the 2009 National Poetry Anthology is a winner in his or her own right. Their poems were selected as winners for their town or area in a free-to-enter annual competition which featured many thousands of entries. The winners are grouped into various regions. If you do not find a winner from your locality this is because insufficient entries were received from that area.

Solomons, London, Adham Smart, Charlton, Paul Jeffery, Harrow, Cathy Mearman, Teddington, Lucy Stubbs, Greenwich, M Lawrance, Englefield Green, Clare Gill, Weybridge, Delsie Barton-Appiah, Mitcham, Dominic Newman, Mitcham, Turid Houston, Ashtead, Iain McGrath, Banstead, Richard J Scowen, Sutton, Marion Griffin, Chichester, Hannah Rose Tristram, Arundel, Beryl Chatfield, Worthing.

SOUTH WEST AND CHANNEL ISLANDS - Pages 71 - 92

Avril Blight, Redruth, Virginia Rabet, Jersey, Sandra Jones, Falmouth, Charlotte Taylor, Truro, Susan Bedford, Exeter, Emily Littler, Torquay, Ralph Scrine, Totnes, Sharon Gordon, Kingsbridge, Katie Mallett, Ilfracombe, Doreen Beer, Exeter, Frank Tout, Torquay, Hilary Jarratt, Kingsbridge, Janet Beardsall, Ottery St Mary, Ted Harriott, Swanage, Debbie Walder, Gillingham, Karlina St Vincent, Highcliffe, Miki Byrne, Tewkesbury, John Head, Alverston, Bob Wilson, Gloucester, Lindsay Sinclair, Bristol, Dora Watkins, Bridgwater, Wendy Paddick, Glastonbury, Martin Perry, Bristol, Peter Prochazka, Bristol, Jo Phillips, Langport, Rosemary Toeman, Porlock, Jo Waterworth, Glastonbury, Peggy Cooper, Highworth, Gill Minter, Chippenham, Kathy Wilson, Devizes.

EAST ANGLIA - Pages 94 - 106

Victoria E Tejedor, Cambridge, Asa Humphreys, Ely, Lindy Jane Rainbow, Ely, Rex Collinson, Cottenham, Derek Lane, Peterborough, Kathryn Aybak, Cottenham, Betty Fenton, Hunstanton, Sylvia Waller, Norwich, John Roebuck, Holt, Charmaine Dunsmore, Kenninghall, Ben Harrison, Great Yarmouth, Jane Dorling, Diss, Marilyn Lyne, Ipswich, Pamela Garrod, Lowestoft, Sarah Caddick, Felixstowe, Carol Shipley, Beccles, Grahame Tanner, Ipswich.

EAST MIDLANDS - Pages 108 - 120

Christine Garner, Chesterfield, Stuart Bunting, Chaddesden, aDele Morgan, Derby, Shilla Mutamba, Coalville, Robert Palmer-Wilson, Leicester, Mo Ward, Hinckley, Rob Adams, Anstey, Julia Knight, Louth, G Merritt, Hardingstone, June Ayling, Weedon Bec, Nadine Platt, Wellingborough, William Shaun Milligan, Corby, Sally Keeling, Towcester, Isobel Burks, Kettering, Bill Hawley, Nottingham, George Shipley, Mansfield Woodhouse, Cheryl Ward, Newark.

WEST MIDLANDS - Pages 122 - 138

Laura Meryl Ross, Hereford, Jenny Renowden, Wythall, Tom Freeman-Keel, Craven Arms, Don Nixon, Albrighton, Dorothy Buyers, Oswestry, Sam Chater, Leek, Phillip Jupp, Uttoxeter, Ben Mcnair, Lichfield, Laura Challinor, Stoke-on-Trent, Lisa Pallin, Stoke-on-Trent, Shirley Wood, Stafford, Jean White, Warwick, Laura Smith, Bulkington, Peter Sammons, Rugby, J Grizzell, Wolverhampton, Margaret Worsley, Coventry, Aradhna Jaswal, Bilston, Jack Kerr, Coventry, Mahmuda Chowdhury, Birmingham, Kenneth Nengovhela, Wolverhampton.

NORTH WEST - Pages 140 - 165

Gay Horton, Macclesfield, Christine Rowley, Winterley, Meg Marsden, Poynton, Dorothea Carroll, Chester, Joshua Brian De Vere, Frodsham, Angela Pritchard, Sandbach, Geoffrey Smith, Carlisle, Linda Dixon, Workington, John Hastings, Workington, Julie Varty, Maryport, Joan Yates, Preston, Troy Tyne, Clitheroe, Rachel Butterworth, Burnley, Stan Frankland, Blackpool, Emma Threlfall, Poulton-le-Fylde, Dave White, Chorley, Marian Barker, Preston, Kathy Denton, Horwich, Rona Catterall, Oldham, Justine A Gibb, Stretford, Cheryl Kelsall, Ashton-under-Lyne, R Crispin, Wigan, Rakiyah Beswick, Stockport, Rachel Martin, Wigan, Elizabeth Gibson, Stockport, Nicola Wilcock, Irlam, Robert

Namushi, Rochdale, Joseph Bailey, Heywood, Wendy Black, Liverpool, Susan Pope, Liverpool, Dorothy Parry, Southport, Ed Collins, Southport.

NORTH EAST - Pages 167 - 197

Janette Coverdale, Middlesbrough, Neil Posselwhite, Loftus, Kathleen Brown, Darlington, Bill Burnett, Stockton-on-Tees, Ann Wilson, Chester-le-Street, David Tobin, Chilton, Lorraine Facey, Crook, Stephanie Gillespie, Durham, Arneil Rutherford, High Shincliffe, Michael Brett, Newbiggin-by-the-Sea, Celia Auld, Ashington, Brenda Thurlbeck, Sunderland, Patrick Brady, Whitley Bay, Eileen Burns, Newcastle-upon-Tyne, Sandi Readhead, Hull, Christine McLaren, Keyingham, Richard Pooley, Hull, Sylvia Varley, York, Margaret Kirkup, Pickering, Vicky Garlick, Ripon, Robert Hill, Ripon, Audrey McIlvain Jefferson, Scarborough, Andrea Mitchell, Thirsk, Barbara Escrick, York, Mark Turvey, Doncaster, Carol Phillips, North Anston, David Jardine, Sheffield, Mary Drost, Halifax, Pauline Hardman, Leeds, Cecilia Brabin, Pudsey, Patricia Farley, Keighley, Suzannah Evans, Leeds, Elaine Bamford, Otley, Barbara Robinson, Boston Spa.

WALES - Pages 199 - 207

Jo Brookes, Newcastle Emlyn, Carolina Rosati-Jones, Swansea, Guy Fletcher, Cardiff, Ken Millard, Newport, Jon Roberts, Holywell, Sarah Williams, Denbigh, Pat Dryden, Holywell, Lynda Howell, Haverfordwest, Arthur Hughes, Llandudno, Ian William Morley, Monmouth, Anne Marie Lawrence, Treorchy, Roger M Robson, Swansea, Riaz Ali, Cwmbran, Sara Reardon, Newport.

NORTHERN IRELAND - Pages 209 - 214

Jennifer Carlisle, Comber, Heather McCracken, Newtownards, Albert Whiteside, Belfast, Ande Milligan, Omagh, William Crawford, Ballywalter, Joan Moore, Londonderry, Betty

McIlroy, Bangor, Pia Gore, Bangor.

SCOTLAND - Pages 216 - 228

Colette Chadha, Gordon, I Elder, Kelso, Ken Angus, Gorebridge, Josephine Duthie, Aberdeen, Hannah Duddy, Glasgow, Tom Guild, Cowdenbeath, Jacqueline Bain, Paisley, Norman Bissett, Edinburgh, Emma Strang, Laurieston, A Harding, Perth, Theresa Bradley Baxter, Motherwell, Britta Benson, Condorrat, Nula Glenn, Dykehead, Arthur Parsons, Coldstream, Muriel Ferrier, Dundee, Lucia Crossan, Glasgow, Ann Odger, Linwood, Grace Tweddle, Crieff, Dina Nicoll, Selkirk.

South
East

13

REVERSING AROUND CORNERS

How many tests is it now?
My drive there is always slightly different,
Even though the result is always the same.

Don't bark at me, I tell him.
He doesn't actually bark,
It's just last minute advice.

He tells me to, *Take a deep breath.*
I remind myself of the hypnotherapy;
Calm, controlled, methodical, relaxed.

I dream about
The new car,
The new job,
All the while, mindful of other road users.

And suddenly we are at the test centre,
I look at the others,
They don't look at me.
We head off, me and the examiner.

Mary McDonnell-Hockley, Shefford, Bedfordshire

FIRE

Ferocious flames flared up
Raging rapidly, right of control
Blazing brightly, billowing in the once dark night
Emitting a warm and inviting glow
Despite the ferociousness, cosy and snug the fire did seem
Excitement soared through each and every soul
It was like a scary, yet enchanted dream
Black smoke enveloped my soul, blackening the very inside
of me
As I walked into the churning mass of smoke

Milly Aziz, Luton, Bedfordshire

STREETLIGHT

It glistens like a turquoise bulb
catching the sunlight.
Making you squint,
protecting your eyes, from the brightness.

Its hood-like shape
distracts you from its base, its holding.

For a while you may wonder,
what this strange shape is.

Dragging your eyes away from the shinning surface,
following the object, top to bottom,
you realise it is a streetlight.

As the sun moves across the sky, you know,
yes, it is a streetlight.

Cheryl Campbell, Luton, Bedfordshire

DEFIANCE

A large black anvil is coming to hammer out the sun
And a glissando of shooting stars flies from the simmering
zenith,
Oblivious to the birds, clap-clapping from the sky in terror.

The kettle ticks as it cools.
The air inside is still, but outside, the fireflies spin around
the trees.
Someone is spattering surrealist monochrome art across
the garden.

The curtains will be closed, but the crackling branches will
not cease
To claw at the windows. Only the wolves will not go into
hiding tonight.

Vanessa Burgar, Ascot, Berkshire

ROUTE 78

It's fine if you keep up,
select your lane and go.

Crouching behind
a rig, big as a house or more.
Its bellow, deep as hell,
won't let you falter.
There's the exit, pull off, slow down,
you're on your own.

It's a delight, the American dream,
mapped in winding tarmac
on green and white,
copsed fields, a clapboard village,
an immaculate church,

Self-contained houses,
flying the stars and stripes,
their manicured lawns
right to the road's edge,
making it hard to stop
and check your way.

Robin Thomas, Reading, Berkshire

THE GREY CHILD OF SEPTEMBER

I am the grey child of September;
No more sparks, just dying embers
And long, diffused shadows.

No strong hues, of orange or red.
Instead the space above the shed
Is filled with the strangest of pinks,

And drinks are taken in the garden,
As the grass grows cold and the hands all harden
And upper arms are hidden.

As unbidden comes the leafy rain
And all the sunlight they contain
Is filtered from the sky.

Clouds no artist would have drawn,
Leaves me feeling somewhat forlorn,
That the shine and sparkles and laughter are gone,

Leaving the comfort of the cool
And the smell of the frost-tinged pool,
As the air comes back to life.

Peter Estdale, Newbury, Berkshire

TIME

Time twists the clock
In the cruel light of day.
Will I ever see you again?
I don't know.

Doubt threatens the future,
Or could it just be fear?
But all we have is the moment,
As you move your pawn.

Say goodbye, before stalemate becomes apparent
And maybe one day, you'll come my way.
So I'll just keep on moving, with your shadow on my
shoulder.
But the feelings may just fade, like a clouded mist at the
start of a new day.

Sarah Palmer, Sonning Common, Berkshire

UNCROWNED QUEEN

The winter's cold is all but nearly spent
And spring's new feelings seethe within the bud.
New juices seep within old thought's intent,
As seasonal rains, the riverbanks flood.
Outgrowing stems anticipate the day
When hawthorn blossoms flower about the hedge,
The harboured sap then fills the leafy spray,
Lost whistling friends bedeck the window's ledge.
In changing skies the songsters spiral
Above the sullen earth where fresh seeds grow;
New aired a wintered love can share a smile,
Reviving all, a brandished dancing show:
Warm sunlight shines on you renewing green,
The earth, the root, the flower, my uncrowned queen.

Geoffrey Allan Taylor, Milton Keynes, Buckinghamshire

19

THE ENEMY

They slandered me, when you had left,
As traitor to my land.
They convict-shaved my long fair hair
And marked me with a brand.

You were the enemy, they said,
Subduing all with threat.
You plundered fields and farms and town,
With deaths they can't forget.

But I have no regrets and guilt
For love I felt for you.
I never saw within your eyes,
A victor's twisted view.

It's gentleness that I recall,
As you made love to me,
The mutual care and peace we felt,
Untouched by war's decree.

My only sadness now is that
You're gone; the war is won
And you will never know you had
A child by me - a son.

Jane Mann, Woodend, Buckinghamshire

DYSLEXIC

A blackened psychology cloak
wears his indifference
and cascades into a backwards
word, blind frenzy,
choking for existence.
Colours bereft of human mankind,
red vibrant of skull-torn crazy,
that mask the satirical soul
And the greys that still remain.

He cowers now,
the lonely sweat of boyhood,
the letters and thoughts
of a poignant childhood,
that dance into a
death bed delusion.
And Satan shakes hands,
announcing the sad schoolboy,
lost of his cue for life.

The cold classroom
cuts the morning air,
the pen and paper
perplex the parody.
He dances and darts
with the devil at dawn.

Mary Mullett, High Wycombe, Buckinghamshire

A NINE 'TIL FIVE

Day the falling, the falling of the morning
Mourn the decay, the sun's aspirations fell away

As the night's coup, the coup of the sun it overthrew
Is such a sight; a sight quelling ambition's hue

A heavy weight, that weighs one down to one such fate
As with the sun, the night renders our dreams undone

Feel the falling, the falling of youth's passions calling
Night breaks the deal; turns hope into something real

A nine 'til five
Chaos' hive and a dreary dive
The sun divine
Can't pierce the mist, its rays can't shine

Goodnight, goodnight. I can't fight the triumph of night
A nine 'til five; I may not thrive but at least I'm alive

Sun's up again
Like a stain, marking a former pain
Let it just fade
For defeat has made me seek the shade

Sean Cable, Milton Keynes, Buckinghamshire

THRALDOM

White and slender is this, as the neck of a swan, yet not so
elegant.
Cursed and abominable, as is the pipe of opium, but does
not so enchant.
A grey wisp rises lazily to disappear, I know not where.
A crimson glow, subdued betwixt the white and grey,
becomes a glare,
Then dies to cause another to rise and melt into the air.
Having offered pleasure, now it takes its toll on all that
dare.
Shortness of cash and breath, the odours of a damp couch
fire,
The fingers yellow-stained, a semblance none desire.
The joy which once it gave, now too late, brings regret,
This damned, accursed, lowly cigarette.

Alan Ellsmore, Andover, Hampshire

PURGATORY

What is the choice that I must face?
How to remove this worthless shell,
Far from the rest of the human race.
A man who never found his place,
Who drank the blood
And relished the taste,
Who took the pain
And shied away,
Only to find
He had lost his faith.
Jesus you cannot save me,
For I married the devil's daughter
And when I cried for you,
She was the only one who came.

Martin McGregor, Andover, Hampshire

DIVERSITY IN NATURE

Small white daisy petals spread upward to the sun.
Buttercup, yellow petals, the sun reflects,
when held beneath the chin for fun.
Tiny pink periwinkles brighten rocky headlands around our
shores and sandy dunes.
Whilst bluebells, in shady glens, dance and play their silent
tunes.
Seas of lemon-headed rape, plump with oil, waiting to be
squeezed, adorn our countryside, along with fields of
lavender containing oil of linseed.
Gardens abound with roses, every colour you can find,
their sweet smelling aromas, soothe tired bodies and
minds.
Delicate white lilies of the ivy, hide its deathly stranglehold
on trees and shrubs.
Vibrant red petals of the poppy, hide its dark secret
which pervades our nightclubs.
Violet shades of deadly nightshade sit silently in our
hedgerows to be admired, but not touched, by those its
secrets know.

Sue Bird, Portsmouth, Hampshire

STORMY WEATHER

The ocean crashed onto the shore,
Moving everything in its pathway,
Thundering along the promenade,
It accompanied the gale's roar.
Mountain-high waves demolished the sea's defences,
Then the onslaught struck once more.

Relentlessly, the sea poured onto the flood plain.
There was the sound of cracking glass.
A newly built house lost a window pane,
The full force of the sea pounded the building
And the glass couldn't take the strain.

The moaning wind moved like an express train.
With a loud bang, a roof lifted high,
Then fell to the earth with a groan.
Nature continued to hold the winning hand
And the wind and rain fed the flowing tide,
Thus extending the danger zone.

Cars and caravans floated in the campsite,
Precious possessions ruined by flood-water.
Too late the storm had reached its height.

Doreen M Bowers, Waterlooville, Hampshire

LANGEMARCK

The tall trees
Provided a gloomy shade
We walked the perimeter
It seemed to be small
For the final resting place
Of twenty-two-thousand soldiers
No headstones
Small stone tablets set in the grass
The improvised crosses of twigs
That the school-children had left
The stillness
The all-pervading silence
The hush when the guns had stopped
The silence that flowed through your being
The peace of these dead

Sean A Gage, Appley, Hampshire

GREY-WOLF

In a wild-open, white, white-wilderness
shadowing in and out of the moon's waking
yellow eyes chill the skin of trees,
mirror the distance of space.

The dark wind is silenced.

Grey-Wolf calls her, howls at the nervous sky
and the slow glide of stars. She answers,
pulses over ground; gathers his scent
slippered across a cold, calloused land.

Clawblades of light
spill over pale scatterings of bone.

Soon, the liquid singing of cubs.

Bridget Joseph, Southampton, Hampshire

GATHERING CLOUDS

The white land cowers, braced
against the distant troughs,
swollen by Atlantic gales,
flung in fury at coastal rocks.

Gusting inland, the wild winter
driven on, the raking rain,
flickering over every pathway;
vivid lightning's dancing flame.

Gathering clouds of rising black,
windy knuckles rapping on doors,
the icy rage breaking windows,
spraying water on kitchen floors.

Bowing trees in bleakness,
cast their shadows on command,
whilst still stalking through the forest,
comes dark winter's unseen hand.

Richard Labram, New Forest East, Hampshire

PRE-EVENT

My flower-girl plays in the corner of the room
Honey-blonde hair, a white t-shirt and shorts
An intent expression of playful concentration
As she shoves her foot with elation
Into an oversized, cerise, suede shoe.
It's mine you know? But what can you do?
Around her everywhere is yet more footwear
Discarded by bridesmaids on the plush cream carpet
While I'm being made up, it's a mess. Shit.
And glossy boxes from boutiques sit
Foaming out tissue like tiny veils

Her perfect white outfit hangs behind her on the door;
White dress, faux-fur stole and tiny white hat
I really can't wait to see her in that
It's almost like she
Is a rehearsal of me
Only a *thousand* times more sweet
But when I take the cerise shoes back
I'm still the one with cold feet

Leila Arshad, Southampton, Hampshire

BANK HOLIDAY BLUES

Where are they dashing to, as they thunder down the
motorway?
The sea, the sea, like lemmings they are dashing to the sea.
They are escaping to their fantasy world.
Where the breezes blow and the sun forever shines.

The waves will crash onto the shore, as before.
Will they arrive before the crowds?
Have they hopefully packed the suncream?
Better take the brolly, just in case.
Summer days have become fickle,
In days of old, the steam-train groaned
And belched smoke as the masses escaped
From drudgery, of the factory floor.
The sun shone brightly in the summer,
Rain came dutifully at night,
In days of yore - not any more.
Now rain will sweep over them all,
Before they reach their Utopian shore.

Betty Shipway, Basingstoke, Hampshire

THE SHORTENING DAYS

Summer, giving way to autumn's heralds.
Balmy evenings, now heavy with chilled dew,
Which settle on once proud heads of fading blooms,
Losing the tints of summer's palette.
Stranded bees, caught unawares, lie dormant.
Their striped thermals sticking damply to their sides,
How wise those bees, safe in their golden combs.
Birds tap on window-panes, bright eyes look in,
Reminding us that food is short. Hang out the nuts
And ham bones filled with juicy marrow.
Hang them high, away from thieving cats.
Sheep, once pink and mottled after shearing,
Now insulated by new, creamy wool,
Later to hang in grey and ochre cords,
Which catch on brambled hedges and barbed wire.
The countryside waits for autumn to bow out
To winter gales and snow; it is prepared,
To fight and to survive until the spring.

June Barlow, Rickmansworth, Hertfordshire

TOMORROW

The end nears and everything is still moving.
My head spins with endless desire,
But for what?
Each day appears before me,
Each day fresh and new.
I wait with anticipation,
Then each day ends.
Today, yesterday,
Has either really passed?
If so, where are my memories?
Where is my joy for another forty-eight hours?
Again, the end nears.
Again, I sit alone,
With nothing but hope,
Yes hope.
And the knowledge,
That tomorrow will soon be here.

John Ryan, Hatfield, Hertfordshire

THE FROST

Beads of glass, on crimson leaves,
Sunlight yawning, through the trees.

Webs of diamonds, lacing stems,
Pronounced against a morbid sky.

Life struggles to survive,
A fist of needles strikes my eyes.

Wendy Harvie, Welwyn Garden City, Hertfordshire

UNICORN

The universe, the alternative universe,
no one walks by, but magic unfolds.
The unicorn, with parchment wings takes flight.
Independent, fearful of the nearness of people who open
her soul, spilling the jewels and gold.

Silent, free, to fly, to be,
over seas and seasons,
will she not grow old?

Scarred by the battles of old acceptance,
skin has grown over, leaving a shadow on once pale, pure,
perfect skin.
Majestic in sleep on golden sand, where fairies blow sleep
breezes over.
The kingdom of the faithful watch over.
Believe in me and you will see through clouds and
darkened skies.

Elizabeth McDonald, St Albans, Hertfordshire

32

AS IF

As if a window came between
The seer and the seen,
A window that is always shut
And will not open out -

I think that once it opened out -

And life is on the other side,
As if at birth I died
And saw a strange procession pass
Before me in the glass.

Is death a breaking of the glass?

Katherine Spiller, Oxford, Oxfordshire

I LOVE YOU WHEN YOU ARE STILL

I love you when you are still, and I
Drink in your profile, in silhouette
Against the dawn-lit, star-faded sky.
I love you when you are still and yet
I fear such stillness, and so caress
Your naked shoulder and watch the rise
And fall of your breast and, seeing, bless
The air you breathe. Fast move your closed eyes
As dreams delight your sleep and make you
Smile, and I pray that I am your dream.
Your skin is pale and, like morning, new.
Your scent as fresh as the rushing stream.

I see your beauty and drink my fill.
Oh, how I love you when you are still.

William Port, Henley-on-Thames, Oxfordshire

33

LOW EBB

I am at a wedding, sent to Coventry.
The cathedral. A quiet corner.
Plopped like a dropped slop in a bucket.
Me, from the wild-Atlantic West,
pumped down a pipe, processed, zoo-ed up,
unsalted, now tasteless, a life-giving waste product,
whose children last only for a day.

Their twenty green stems are probing me where it hurts,
poles of super-lilies. I caress their legs,
lapping my stillness over their sapping stilts.
Like me, they're going nowhere.

At least they can see over the top,
But they're looking away.
Not even a flower wants to be a wallflower,
Even water disdains tears.

Joanne Mosley, Abingdon, Oxfordshire

CARBON BONDING

We touch the scrolled frond
of your spine, blow on your sealed eye,
study the dark that surrounds you
in the scan: the cavern of black water or oil,
and, beyond, the press
of coal, peat, settling leaves.

Janet Irving, Radley, Oxfordshire

THE MONTH OF MAY

Is May the best of months?
When Mother Earth's seed quickens,
Her warming breath thaws,
Wakening the sleeping land,
Dispelling winter's cold dreams.
Her life blood swells the thickening bud
That spills the fruitful blossom,
To ripen into summer fruits,
Under a prosperous sun.
The rich humus bright
And alive now with swathes
Of flowers, their gentle
Faces lifted by the softening wind
And the birds unto the heavens, call
With sweet voice, sing loud
In praise the psalms of spring.

Richard Dixon, Benson, Oxfordshire

SINGING

To sing my songs in minor keys
of darkest nights, of sunless days,
I'd need to tell how misted skies
dampen views and bring a maze
to cloud my thoughts, so colour flies.

There would be no light to flame,
to fire with golden glow my words.
How dull the music, so composed,
how lifeless and unstressed the chords,
how out of tune, with meaning closed.

But if a major key I choose,
a key with tone to lift and lighten,
I could sing of sunkissed days
and silver skies at night to brighten,
Earth then would hear these rainbow lays.

So hope and scintillating life
would stir the air and truly take
all the singing strains to heart.
A merry music there could make
coloured words, and grace impart.

Michaela Davis, Witney, Oxfordshire

THE UNDERGROUND

The tube is full.
The grey upright pensioner
Reviewing the advertisements -
That's me.
Silently
I sit
Hands folded, body still.

The hurricane within
Continues, unabated
Shaking, shattering
Sheering, breaking.

The shell holds.
No fragment escapes
To challenge the shapes
Of your reality.

Tell me,
What's the weather like in you?

Susan Stead, Headington, Oxfordshire

SILVER JUBILEE TRAIN

A necklace of light in the darkness,
Far away over the hill.
A whistle that pierces the distance,
When all around you is still.

A rumble that grows to a thunder,
A chaos of racket and light,
This riveting creature's upon us,
A train through the depths of the night.

A monster of smooth, shining metal,
Of silver and trembling power,
It rivals the wind in its swiftness
At full eighty miles to the hour.

In the carriages people are reading
Or just sitting quietly, thinking.
In a flash all excitement is over
And now we have time to recover.

A fading, red, rearlight is winking,
Then peace on the empty steel rail.

Marjorie Inkster, Bampton, Oxfordshire

CHANGING

Whenever I started speaking
You changed the subject
My words
Faltered
Into silence

Two suitcases, a train
Life in the fast lane
Money in the bank
A cat called Frank
New clothes, new hair
A torrid affair
Campaigning for a cause
A holiday in Oz
Yoga, Tai Chi
Earl Grey tea
A smart new
Chic new
Brand new me

Now I return
We sit, I speak
And once again
You change the subject

Jennifer Russell, Chinnor, Oxfordshire

SUCCUMBED TO DEATH OF DARKNESS

Sun will set soon, day replaced by ghostly moon,
Hopeful head peers out of the door to see the soldiers leave
Or my lover come to me once more.

The door must reveal her, worries disappear
And I can tell her more,
I am on the run from the men of law.

They track me through day and night, never do I disappear
or fight,
They come tonight and break through
Kill with fear of fright.

Promises she made, by midnight here she would be,
Even if she comes fast, she will be beaten
And I will not last.

The flames flicker, I hadn't thought they'd arrive quicker.
A rustle by the gate, my time is up,
My life is but fate.

Knocking at the door, once, twice, thrice then four,
I ran out the back gate,
Fled where my lover wouldn't find me, I knew not she was
arriving late.
I had succumbed to death of darkness.

Ciaran McCormick, Southend-on-Sea, Essex

DOWN INTO A BLACK CAB PARKED

Down into a black cab parked
alongside a gnarly old tree.

The tree was the last thing I saw.
The shadows that fell on it told me
the sun was going down,
but I couldn't see it.
There was a blue wreath of mist
And the tree shrank from it,
but couldn't escape.
It curled its fingers around it and held on for
dear life
and I wished I could.

Down into a black cab,
down, down.

Rebecca Hastie, Little Horkesley, Essex

VICTORIA CIRCUS

In sun-drenched rainlight glimpsed through glass,
I preserve them, fragile specimens of a time and place,
A fragment of a Thursday afternoon
Populated by butterfly people on tissue paper wings,
In purses, coffee cups, plastic bags and puddles.

Here and now with molten heart and leaping blood, hands
twitching to enfold,
Logos and faces suspended in a sky that takes me by
surprise,
The purchase-pulse of shopping bags asway
To skinny-jeans synchronicity, the rhythm of the afternoon.

This is all, reality is the outline of a laugh the wind whips
loose into the beating pulse, a heartbeat passed
And grey transmuted into gold.

In glass I preserve them, fragile specimens of a time and
place,
A fragment of a Thursday afternoon,
A life in latte-froth,
An era in the rattle of receipts.

Josie Turner, Benfleet, Essex

THE BENCH

Here, in this place,
Shrubs of evergreen
Cocoon the space
And enclose the bench
With a frothy screen.

In twilight he arrives,
A hunk in rags,
On scraps he survives
Disposed by the bench,
In crumbled up bags.

Bewhiskered and weathered
And covered in sores,
From society severed.
Deposed on the bench,
He lives outdoors.

Newspaper for a sheet,
Cardboard for a quilt,
It is here he will sleep,
Dozed on the bench,
On the bed he has built.

Jessie Whitman, Wickford, Essex

LOST

She stands on the beach, the wind in her face.
She watches the boats, their sails taut as they tack close to
the shore.
Does she see them?
Her dark eyes are watchful,
Her dark hair in two long plaits framing her quiet face.
Long floral skirt blowing against her tanned legs,
She holds an apple in her hand.
Who is it for?
I know, I know her, I know how she has suffered.
I know her loss.
Does she see the boats? Does she see the world?
She will quite soon.
She is coming back to us.
The sea and the wind and the empty sky will help to make
her whole again.

Jill Stearn, Colchester, Essex

WILDING TREE

To Wilding Tree we will walk
Just you and me
By the roadside, we will talk
At Wilding Tree.

We will see the silent pool
Just you and me
Join the bark with canine call
At Wilding Tree.

We will come back home again
From Wilding Tree
To the land of dogs and men
Just you and me.

Alan Dickson, Rochester, Kent

THE SPELL

Their arms entwined, their heads inclined,
They walked the path that led along
The ancient, unused cart-track way,
Through herb-strewn fields to Avignon.

The air was still, the close-knit pair,
Half bewitched, with footsteps slow,
Slipped through a copse of ivied trees
And found the ruined, old chateau.

They might have stepped into the past,
So wildly beautiful the scene.
The very ruins seemed to speak,
Perhaps to plead for what had been.

The broken windows looked upon
A crystal lake as clear as day
And on it glided two black swans,
Close, enchanted, just as they.

Then, as they stood bemused and still,
The great birds rose from off the lake.
It broke the spell, they homeward turned,
The silence deepening in their wake.

Gwen McIntyre, Eynsford, Kent

FOOTPRINTS

I have left my footprints
Wet upon the sand,
Imprinted deep and clear, defined
Just as I wish to leave
a memory, engrained
Upon the minds
Of loved ones left behind
And yet
All thoughts of me will fade,
By passing time, I fear;
As prints upon wet sand are set
So soon to disappear

Ann H Pinder, Snodland, Kent

HYTHE ACCENTS

In mid-spring the pink cherry and white almond trees
blossom like wedding lollipops, green swathes lead to
mottled grey waters. How serious.
Town's thoughts gather; shoppers, children dogs, cats,
empty milk bottles by doorsteps, bright clothes and ill
fitting rags gazing into windows, bosomy matrons,
skinny teenagers, loud boys enjoying the hubbub all.
The old bread shop like the Red Lion Square, where lovely,
warm and so-called *real bread* was sold for pennies.
I mustered a whole load once for the ducks, but they
thought it too opulent and paddled away.
The roads are slidey, little patterns of streets that touch
and go round matronly corners where the dark houses spill
into a shoppy front, people everywhere.
Saturdays bustling and the Red Cross shop where I met
someone.
There are many secret ways getting to know those who live
in the stories that abound, a good place to start.
Quaint prayers, monuments to future past.

Simon Partridge, Dover, Kent

NAVY

It was there I took cover, though yet to discover vacuity
As it were, I bemused, in a room diffused with silence,
The colour of navy
For black alone means something shone
But something, underneath the none, awaited my entrance

And it seemed I heard it prattle this way
Until, of course, my on-my-way
Forewarned it, *Halt, hide away!*
But my intrusion did not prove, inconclusive, that I intrude
I was a welcomed guest there

There I became an apparatus with no name, anonymous
As it were, less confused in a room without clues
For the silence, the silence, synonymous
Something meant that time was spent
Something underneath the nothing,
Prepared me for this event

And it seemed I felt a hand in mine
An assuring touch of, *never you mind*
Forewarning me that, *Soon it is time*
Time for the conversion of blue to black
'Til nothing is beneath the something
Inevitably, nothing, beneath the something

Sheila Brown-Ellis, Deal, Kent

BALLOON

often on those evenings balloons would bubble up
low in the sky and small and pale at first
above the pale hills

growing and darkening as they approached
between glances they shifted unaccountably
dipped behind trees
reappeared

though sometimes seeming bound to reach us
always they would veer away
suddenly small again
suddenly gone for good

but late in the season
late in the day
that time when it was just the two of us
one came and from the first it did not swerve
until it loomed above and then descended
landing full-square on the common
with none of the usual disarray

and when that man got out and strode towards us
for a moment I imagined him ethereal ambassador
and I was ready to obey

Jonathan Overell, Snodland, Kent

KEATS THE CHEMIST

Behind the counter in a chemist's shop
I found John Keats. The poet was on fire.
Consumption, that would bring him to a stop,
Burned urgently, but it could not aspire
To rival flames the Muses set alight
And in his incandescent eyes, I saw
The fire-storm of desire burn yet more bright
For Fanny Brawne, such was the torch he bore.
I turned to go. I heard the poet sigh.
What masterpiece I'd flawed, I dared not think.
I looked back from the door, I saw one eye
Obliterated in a monstrous wink.
I quaked. He ventured, *May I recommend*
These requisites Sir, for a long weekend?

Charles Wright, Westgate-on-Sea, Kent

THE THREAD

The thread on which the issue hangs is fine
As gossamer, that breaks on instant touch,
Or scatters to the winds of chance. The line
To which the toes are tipped, is not so much
As drawn for eager eyes to see, or hands
To grasp, but makes as sure a groove to feel,
As lines that space the equatorial lands
Divide the regions of our turning wheel.

Perhaps the sum of all our learning is
To weigh the balance drawn from this and that,
Not to stage a universal quiz
Composed of welder, linesman, acrobat,
For though the seed with tender care is sown
The final harvesting is never known.

Mary Nugent, Whitstable, Kent

49

INVOCATION TO THE MOON

In piercing global warming heat
I wandered from the city street
And in the quiet, cool gallery
I felt your presence soothing me,
A soft, cool ointment gently flowing
Around my thoughts in beacons glowing.

I stayed, where from the painting you
Shone, on the woods as I came through
The canvas and the leafless trees
And felt your cool beams in the breeze
And all the burns on skin and soul,
Healed with the air and o-zone hole.

Comforted in your silver seas
Of moonlight, from among the trees,
I ask that all your soft, clear rays
Fall on the atmospheric blaze
And from the painting, where you glow,
Receive the world, refreshed by snow.

Robert Duncan Martin, Canterbury, Kent

SPRING

Spring is coming, but not quietly,
Instead, in a fanfare, a cacophony
Of wind like an express train

Roaring past trembling window panes,
Blasting errant bumble bees
Against the glass, sorry refugees

Beaten and lashed with rain,
Never to see home again.
There are *rivers* running past my door,

I haven't seen those before.
And water cascades from every roof,
These urban waterfalls are surely proof

That something worse is still to come
In time and in some
Ways we cannot guess,

And yes,
Nature, the nurturer, become the abused,
Is in breakdown mode and very confused.

Jacqueline Cooke, Bexleyheath, Kent

GAP YEAR

My friend the tramp
Says he's on his gap year,
I'm not sure from what.

He says he's using it to travel
But he just seems to hang around Camden.

He says he's improving his people skills,
He might brush up on IT,
He seems to be serious.

Says he's finished with Marxist dialectics
And is looking into a safe investment
That will give him a steady return
On his capital,
He's only got a shopping trolley
And a collection of old tube maps.

He's asked for a written introduction
To any captains of industry
Of my acquaintance,
I really don't know any.

I've given him the address of a good drop-in centre
But he doesn't seem interested

Raymond Blake, London, Greater London

WINDS OF TRUTH

I want love, pure and simple.
No dramatics or Greek tragedies,
No epics of Latin mysteries.
Just sweet sensations and delicious communion.

Sweet lingering kisses with no shadow passing through.
Half-rated, semi-cemented histories,
Creeping in to paradise.
Liquid slime, corroding the fantasy.
I have dug a trench, to ensure what I deserve,
Truth, love and sincerity are my sun, wind and earth.

Isabel Tepper, London, Greater London

THE THAMES

Moneyed prophets own the quays
Your pensioned roar when moons recede
Reflects the, *me first,* city mood
The twilight makes a feisty duel

Upon the municipal grail's greasy spill
And all the black bits from the mill
Commuters through embankment take
The river and its filtered stake

That wrestles with an Appoline lilt
Whose Dionysian colours built
A bridge or two, a crown estate
Hesitant but never late
The Thames

Eddie Saint-Jean, London, Greater London

BLUSHES OF INNOCENCE

Full of life and charm,
This sweet rose blushes like
A virgin, so innocent, so shy
Who once wed her besotted prince.

To fulfil his dreams
She bore him two sons;
An heir to the throne, she did provide,
Our future, joy and pride.
A superb royal mother to become.

Without hesitation, with devotion
And verve, she lavished her maternal love
On everyone, this nation and the world.

Why not treat her to a larger than life-size
Statue, so the light of her gorgeous face
Shines upon us and she smiles at us a smile

Of warm affection to fill all hearts
With hope, to calm this violent London down,
To work magic and save lives of the young,
To inspire all to follow her path?

Lucy Carrington, London, Greater London

INSOMNIAC

Oak panels propel
the listener to press
an ear to the wall.

Something safe about wood,
the way it admits
subtle sound waves

to seep unnoticed
through knots
in the timber.

He can't move;
transfixed, he warms
to the music;

not the words
but the cadences,
the knowledge that someone else

is alive and normal,
mouthing their thoughts
out loud in the dark.

Isabella Mead, Bethnal Green, London

MEMORIES

They emerge with unexpected vigour
Like in a child's kaleidoscope
With colours, sharp and bright
And time with grace surrenders to the future
You are young and free again
You feel the summer meadow
The wind caressing you
And blossoms bow in gentle adulation

Possibilities colour
Your skies an endless blue

And then you sense the dimming
The fading into grey
Cracks cutting an encroaching net
Uniting with splintering disintegration

A thousand little shards leave you in blinding white

Veronica Marsh, London, Greater London

DO NOT LOVE ME

Do not love me as you love your computer
booting me up, jabbing with your fingers
leaving me to grow cold in the night.

Do not love me as you love your television,
spending warm, hilarious evenings, eating
and drinking in my company, then ignoring me
all day, drawn to the gaze of every other television
in shops and other houses.
Then coming home to turn me on.

Do not love me as you love and hate your car
discharging all your anger inside me
as we push through the crowded world, cursing
slamming my door with relief
marching away from me to relax.

Love me as you love your mobile.
Keep me with you always.
Respond to me immediately.
In idle moments, turn to me, cradle me
gaze at me.
Sleep with me.

Penny Solomons, London, Greater London

LOCK CHASE, SE3

The death of daylight
over mossy roofs. Dying
sunlight, pre-nightfall.

The trees have muscles -
apple, pine. Their smells: notes of
pure bass, brown, brown, brown.

Sodium sprinkles
onto cropped grass-filament
corrosiveness.
Electrons wash over me,
stroke me, like incense smoke,
soft against my skin.

The dancing trees.
The lichen on the breezeblocks.
The blanket of sky.

The death of daylight
over roofs of clay. Flying low,
the helicopter.

Adham Smart, Charlton, Greater London

A SEASIDE MOURNING

The mourners tread the path the widow paves,
Eradicate the words they wrote in sand
As haunting ghosts, benevolent or knaves.

Some truly sad, some frozen mid the graves,
Some grim but uniformed they stand;
These mourners tread the path the widow paves.

Respect all show, deep reverence one saves,
With glove in glove or maybe hand in hand
Like haunted ghosts, benevolent or knaves,

Away from organ, semi-breve and staves,
To what will lie forgotten on the strand
Like flotsam warped by passing years and waves.

Yet memorising merely makes us slaves
To thoughts at once both reverent and bland
Of haunting ghosts, benevolent or knaves.

The aching heart some soured solace craves,
From rivals, friends, a sinister, dark band
Of mourners on the path the widow paves;
She haunts these ghosts, benevolent or knaves.

Paul Jeffery, Harrow, Greater London

VIOLIN GIRL

The girl is of Irish descent,
Curvy shoulders, dark flowing hair.
She looks out to the ocean,
Her thoughts are in motion;
What song will she sing?

A ballad or a lament,
Strung on the violin?
Songs that will be heard across the sea,
Soaring on wings of destiny,
In the land of her birth.

Cathy Mearman, Teddington, Greater London

SPENDTHRIFT

What I would now give
To be with you
A few moments of time
To hear the softness of your voice
To see your tall frame stooped in a doorway
To lap up your shy effacing smile
To take in your wild, black hair.
All those years you were alive
I was a spendthrift with time
And frittered it away.

Lucy Stubbs, Greenwich, Greater London

ARRIVAL OF SPRING

It's here, I know I saw it,
First tiny buds of spring,
Bright green on gaunt and naked trees.
Nature's humble offering.

It's here, I know I smelt it,
Those woody, mossy scents,
Carried on gentle breezes
With winter's harsh consent.

It's here, I know I heard it,
Nesting birds call loud,
Seeking new mates for the year,
So courageous and so proud.

It's here, I know I feel it,
The warmth flows through my veins.
Hope is born in every spring,
When life starts once again.

M Lawrance, Englefield Green, Surrey

SAVAGE SUN

Midday hangs in a stifling, airless sky,
On this, another record-breaking August scorcher.
Dusty, fissured roads reach ahead
towards shimmering lakes in infinity.
Watery oases held eternally unobtainable
as the illusion slides ever beyond.
Weeping asphalt forms glutinous, tarry puddles
of inky-black, glimmering, rainbow, diamonds.

Only the heat sidles skywards at any pace.
Time suspended,
still any inner-drives to apathy.
Existence - lifeless, crisp, withered,
by the sun's merciless glare.
Sultry heat and dust
linger in today's ferocious oppression
beneath our savage sun.

Clare Gill, Weybridge, Surrey

DEAD

I'm not supposed to be here.
I had to try to save her, didn't I?
Failed; too weak.
Her hand brushed mine and for a second everything was
alright.
But the water, the current, whatever it was, tore at me,
lashing, holding me, chaining me down.

It was dark. Then I saw her. Then dark.
Is she alright? Did she get out?
She's not here.
That's great, that's good. I'm glad for her.

They're taking me home.
Here's my car,
It's nice; black, sleek yet hunchbacked.
This is my ending,
But I'm not supposed to be here.

Delsie Barton-Appiah, Mitcham, Surrey

REFUGE IN SUBURBIA

At last, he can be far away from London's dreary working
day.
He leaves behind strip-lighting's glare; he flees from
artificial air.
At last, his soul is now his own: no more automaton or
clone.
He plunges through the traffic's soar; begins, as many
times before,
his journey to suburbia.

He enters London Waterloo in time to catch the quarter-to.
He boards it; chooses to ignore the station's vast, celestial
roar;
His train pulls out towards his home, through London's
dingy honeycomb.
He's left at a bland, lifeless station, where roofs peek over
vegetation -
the city's home: suburbia.

While sodium orange fills the streets, he homeward plods
his way, and greets
each paving stone with tired eyes.
His homely front door he espies
and, coming slowly back to life, embracing now his waiting
wife.
At last, at last, he can be free. He shuts the door, and,
suddenly,
there's refuge in suburbia.

Dominic Newman, Mitcham, Surrey

FIREFLIES

The luminescent beetle that was caught
within my two clasped hands would grant, you said,
my wish. But you, that Tuscan night, had brought

such turmoil to my soul that my poor head
could think of no sagacious wish. And so
my fevered brain spawned wishes that instead

were all too earthy for his magic glow
and too abstruse in their intensity
to heap on his bright wings. I let him go,

unburdened. *He* knew what his course must be:
His insect yearning, simple and entire,
was for the wingless glow-worm, urgently.

And trailing phosphorescence of desire
into the night he danced, his heart afire.

Turid Houston, Ashtead, Surrey

BONFIRE NIGHT

On a black canvas,
Rockets scream, dogfight for space and attention.
Short-fused egos sparkle, give no quarter, until
In a migraine of air-bursts, they self-destruct,
Spiting themselves like spoiled children.

A Catherine wheel squares up
To three Roman candles,
Like a frenzied peacock, it spits defiance with random
precision,
Rainbowed in sparks, they yield.

Little children, necks craned, gaze wide-eyed,
Pupils eager for the carnage above,
Gnawing absently at toffee apples.

Aloof from such pyrrhic victories,
Just one survivor,
A sooty guy, sitting on a wooden throne
Awaiting his fifteen minutes of flame.

When his turn comes, both sides have retired,
Defeated, to rest and lick their wounds.
This battle is over, but the star wars will go on.
Next year.

Iain McGrath, Banstead, Surrey

THE PARTING

On that cold platform, we stood in
Silence, each of us - that tomb-like day.
Our spring had been so brief,
All too soon, your suitcase packed
With crushed memories.
Time, the eternal thief.

You said, *I really cared for you,*
Or so I thought you did.
A hair's breadth from parting,
Your train draws near, I weep.
Will there be a letter from you?
Or does love shrivel in its final sleep?

You sat in silence, neither kiss nor word,
You staring ahead, the carriage
Door slams hard; our farewell brief.
The whistle blows, the train moves on
And spirits you away like
Some infernal thief.

Richard J Scowen, Sutton, Surrey

THE PENNY WHISTLE

Don't put your penny whistle away
Just because they said you couldn't play
Without a licence
But you need an address for a licence
You need money for a licence
And you have neither of these
They were deaf to your pleas
To be allowed to play
And not put your penny whistle away

As you leave through the park, those who sit
On the benches and walk around a bit
Will hear your music
Children on the swings will hear your music
Lovers in the grass will hear your music
To comfort the lonely and sad
And give joy to all to make them glad
That you played once more that day
Before putting your penny whistle away

Marion Griffin, Chichester, Sussex

POSTCARD TO JOE

Roll with me in the heather and heath
Breathe with me by the rocks
Wash with me in the waters
Feel the loosing of locks

For I am sent out full of spirit
The winds of the earth are my breath
If you've something to sing, I shall hear it
Sweet man I'll hold dear beyond death

Hannah Rose Tristram, Arundel, Sussex

THE TIDELESS SEA

Wind rustles the trees, the clock ticks,
Pulse beats are steady and calm, and breathing slows;
The curtain of night falls and peace descends
Like soft eiderdown quilt, smothering sounds.

Cars distantly pass and rain falls,
Swift lightning splits the sky, without thunder.
Darkness dims the world and blurs its edges,
The power to move is lost, awareness wakes.

Is this the gate of heaven, nirvana now? -
Where nothing shall afright or cause alarm,
But brooding silence recreates the soul
And mystery of creation is made known.

Infinity of space is strangely home
And time gives away to quiet expanding joy;
Earth's problems fade before eternity,
Lost in a tideless sea of endless love.

Beryl Chatfield, Worthing, Sussex

South West

THE STONE

It stands unchanging through the year, yet in the spring
I look upon this stone, surrounded as it is with
Daffodils, cream primroses and their bright new leaves
And think then of another, in another place, another time.
This stone, a living life force, speaks of that third day
When rolled away from empty tomb, the other then
Revealed a timeless truth which on this Easter morn
Is manifest in its simplicity.
Look on the stone and for a fleeting moment,
See eternity.

Avril Blight, Redruth, Cornwall

THE GIRL FROM RENNES

I saw her sitting cross-legged,
Upon a grey cobbled street in Rennes.
As her weary head lifted slowly,
Her smoky blue eyes held mine.
I felt the deep sadness within her,
Her transient beauty held no bounds.
Woollen shawl draped over her shoulders,
A thin, faded, patched dress covered her form.
A dog sat beside her, quiet and still,
Her sadness transmitted through to him.
Its old weary bones not moving at all,
Little brown dog curled up in a ball.
People dropped money into her lap,
While the girl played her flute to tune.
Her heart and soul were in another place,
As her ethereal music held passers by.
She sat on that cold, cobbled street,
Her old flute echoing enchanting music.
Stooped on her shoulders, lay the world,
That beautiful young girl, from Rennes.

Virginia Rabet, Jersey, Channel Islands

LADY IN WHITE

Soft music and laughter in the air, coloured lanterns gently swaying in the trees
The gent in the top hat and tails serenading, his words of love carried on the breeze
His melodious voice captivating, enthralling the dancers of the night
As she walked down the steps of the hall there were gasps at the Lady in White
Her luxurious gown of silk and satin, her dark hair entwined with pearls
Her beauty like a Grecian goddess, nymph-like she danced and twirled
As she relaxed and drank champagne, the moonlight lit up her face
Her dark eyes so sad and wistful, her fragility seeking solace
Dreamy, romantic and languid, to absorb, to remember, to forget
Melodic music lulling you to obscurity, seemingly endless thoughts of regret
With memories of war, long-forgotten, on a hot, sultry summer's night
A will-o'-the wisp, as if acquainted, blew a kiss to the Lady in White

Sandra Jones, Falmouth, Cornwall

CHOOSING TO BARE THE PAIN

I'm holding on by a tiny thread
To a relationship that's feeling half-dead
Why can't it be plain-sailing?
Not free-falling
Just floating on a whisper of love

I choose to bare the pain between us
Because I know we can see through the problems
And find the light at the end of it all
No matter how small it is

We can fly to our destined world
Where dreams are real
And our spirits are free

Charlotte Taylor, Truro, Cornwall

CREDITON JUNCTION

The Lady Margaret of Looe Valley
Waits at the crossing in Crediton.
The driver talks to the signalman
As day closes;
A moment
Caught
Between
Day and night,
Between
Staying and leaving,
Between
Railway and road,
Friendship between men;
A working man's smile.

Susan Bedford, Exeter, Devon

WEDDED BLISS

We are getting old apart, you and I.
You sit with your eyes shut as I watch on by.
I watch as you throw yourself into the deep end;
You depend on me,
But I'll let you down.

I'm a mess, You confess, *But my heart still is pure.*
I'd like to contend that, I'm not quite so sure,
Your hairline's receding, your footprints misleading,
The garden needs weeding, You look at me pleading,
But I don't want to do it.

Wedded bliss is over-rated,
Just like tofu, sex and children.

I feel no affection in your direction and this reflection leads
me to the question, *Just why am I here at all?*
But I know why,
I am just as bad.
We are getting old apart, you and I,
But together we'll manage just fine.

Emily Littler, Torquay, Devon

MEETING FOR LUNCH

Her room is locked when I get there.
I leave my card
and ask in all the usual places,
but no one has seen her.

I sit on a hard bench,
clasping my cap on my knee
like some lost traveller at Waterloo.

The young flow round me,
ascending to fast-food luncheons,
or settling in pairs to unpack
plastic protected sandwiches.

I try not to look
conspicuously elderly.

But, I am alone
and, for a moment,
frightened.

Ralph Scrine, Totnes, Devon

RAIN

With hail and thunder you rage
but with tiny drips you nurture
the small flowers that suckle from the moisture
that then trickles down the drain
or to a nearby stream
and flows effortlessly
to sustain life;
bathing, nourishing
encouraging both
the big and tall
weak and vulnerable.
I feel ashamed that I complain
when you trickle down
my window.

Sharon Gordon, Kingsbridge, Devon

MOUSE

I thought I'd cornered you, your pointed nose
And whiskers hardly twitching as you froze
Beside the door frame, shiny black lead eyes
Scanning your escape. You were my prize
My crane-claw fingers could have closed around
Your trembling shape, an insignificant mound
Of fluff. But suddenly it seemed you saw
My shadow, like a giant wing or paw
About to pounce. You sprang and moved so fast
I hardly saw you run, a blur that passed
My toes to somewhere hidden. I couldn't wait
To rid myself of you with traps and bait.
But when I found you dead, stretched out as though
You'd leapt towards your fate, how could you know
I wept, and wished I could have let you go?

Katie Mallett, Ilfracombe, Devon

FINALE

A flash of ultimate brilliance briefly bedazzled all,
Instantly, blindfoldingly, sight was banished, brains
befuddled.
Trees heaved anchored roots and rose like ashen ghosts,
Defoliated and desiccated.
Rivers left their courses, boiled over twisted rail tracks
And along melting motorways.
Micro-waved fish tossed lifelessly in the molten effluvium,
Featherless flyers plummeted and were engulfed.
Saps, plasmas and lifebloods amalgamated,
Animal, vegetable and mineral compounded.
Sahara, Simpson and Atacama,
Sand-stormed simultaneously and intermixed
And continents were not.
Dust to dust and ash to ash,
A blackness descended.
For one world, one play, the final act staged,
The curtain fallen,
There was no encore.

Doreen Beer, Exeter, Devon

MELT

Light as air on cantilevered wings, bright as sunshine on
tinted chrome,
Drowned out in silence by the melody she sings, her voice
shall echo you home.
The sky is full of white horse clouds, galloping towards the
moon,
Manes flying like whispered silk, against a backdrop of
deep maroon
And at night sky carries the pure-bred stock, the falling
night at dawn.
From the gelding's young stance, to the dapple's fetlock,
A new breed of sky horse is born.
Ride this thoroughbred steed on the wind, to the birth of
this new day.
Lightness falls around like a yellow veil,
Leaving all stone blind within its shell.
Hearts and flowers riding on a crest of morning's call,
Remembering her perfume so very well.
In a field of special moments, cast in passion and pain,
Lust formed in fire, love born in rain,
So warm and inviting,
Her smile can melt you down.

Frank Tout, Torquay, Devon

FULL MOON AT SUNSET

At the end of the day, I stood
In a rising field and saw
A blood-red moon escaping from the sea.
She hung like a Chinese lantern
Smiling at me.
And then I turned and saw
From that same spot, her image
Double-red, falling into a distant land
Burning with gold and fire.
O' many a time have I looked in vain
For that one magic moment.
Just to be there, and see again
A full and rising moon
And setting sun, together.

Hilary Jarratt, Kingsbridge, Devon

STOPPING ON THE JOURNEY

On walks he always stopped
To look at other things:
Birds, trees, butterflies and the sky.
He pottered round his garden.
Studying flowers, insects, growth and decay
And never failed to look up at
The moon and stars at night.
He lingered to look at sunsets,
Hills and valleys, blue-grey in the mist.
The scent of every flower he adored
And polish, cut grass, freshly laundered sheets.
He much preferred to stay and chat awhile to
Anyone, especially those he loved.
His journey was a joyful thing, with many
Halts along the way. He enjoyed it all:
Far more than his destination.

Janet Beardsall, Ottery St Mary, Devon

THE WARRIORS RETURN

Somewhere between my imagination and my ears
I can almost hear their chirruping fanfares
From high above some distant ocean
Calling us to welcome them home.
Though these brave armies of the airwaves,
Who fight their Battle of Britain
Twice every year,
Will barely be acknowledged
Or gain any applause,
Theirs is a tale of everyday wonder.

The world's greatest explorers,
Who make their incredible journeys without maps,
Will soon be swooping low over the cliffs again
To herald the joy season with their song.
A light in each eye and a swelling of every breast
Should make us doubt our definitions of courage;
Frown over our endless celebration of ancient heroes
And feel humble before the martins,
Though there should be
No laurel wreaths for them.

Ted Harriott, Swanage, Dorset

THE HEALER

Time wrapped its healing bandages around my broken
heart.
It bathed my wounds in soothing balm, told sadness to
depart.
They tell you, *Life goes on my friend, look to the future, not
the past,*
Enjoy each day as if it was your first and then your last.

Relationships bring suffering, with doubt and fear and woe,
To crush a petal in your hand, instead of letting go.
Dark nights bring long and lonely hours, disturbed by
dreams of terror,
With acid thoughts that poison me and spark the
smouldering fire.

Thoughts in my head go round and round, caught in a
ferris wheel.
Distorted images, mirrors of life, confuse the way I feel.
Have the years been wasted or have the lessons been
learned?
Habits and mistakes repeated, the scalding wound is
burned.

Debbie Walder, Gillingham, Dorset

LINKED

I know the hills and valleys
Of your voice,
The rushing waterfalls
Of enthusiasm and enterprise.
The dull, slow beat
Of thudding head or heart,
The fine edge changes
In mood or mind.
And like a barometer
You register the pressure
Of my days;
Note the north wind's adversity,
Warm a chill moment
Of my life
With your certainty
Of fair weather to come.
Thoughts, ideas, emotions, events,
Words crowd the phone line,
Eating the miles, stopping the gaps,
Blessedly linking our lives.

Karlina St Vincent, Highcliffe, Dorset

BEST VIEW

A white plastic chair, boring and ordinary
With grass climbing about its legs.
Strategically placed for the best view of the paddock.
It has been there for some time,
It's ingrained with mould and grime.

Yet this chair has held the parents,
Watching as their offspring ride,
Has heard the gasps, the encouragement shouted,
The admonitions and the proud sighs.

Whilst in the paddock, horses trot
With young enthusiasts on their backs,
All yearning for mum and dad's attention;
Praise for their skills
And a kindly ignoring of what they lack.

Poor old chair, so bleak when empty.
Simply a product of tacky, mass-production,
But there a throne of hope and pride,
Best seat in the house as they watch the children ride.

Miki Byrne, Tewkesbury, Gloucestershire

LARK PLUMMETS

Lark plummets
in diminishing crescendos,
a dying flame of song,
linking the ages with
repeated ecstasies.

Always, too,
the cry of the martyr
reverberates in consciences,
posing irresistible questions.

Always, too, questioning teachers
disturb sand gardens
of complacencies.

Always, too, the saviour
presents eternal inconsistencies.

Still song dwindles
to grassy silences
but, responsive to new dawnings,
ascends to fresh,
triumphant harmonies.

John Head, Alveston, Gloucestershire

WHISPERING WOOD

A blue sky reigns
As hand in hand
We meander along
The grassy tracks that
Lead to *Nell's Dark Wood.*
In the whispering gloom
Of a pine-scented glade
She firmly presses her
Glossy lips on mine.
Green tufted grass, like a
Soft woollen carpet, supports
Our bony, naked frames
That rise and dip again and
Again in powerful harmony.
Then, the animal frenzy
Over, we move slowly
Into the shadowy light
Of evening, hands clasped
Even tighter than before.
Beaming, beautiful smiles.

Bob Wilson, Gloucester, Gloucestershire

PASSENGER OF TIME

I'm not just a passenger in your car
Travelling this conveyor-belt road
I'm a passenger in your life
A little more weight on your burdened load

When you're ready, you'll stop like a bus
Waiting and watching me leave
Time for me to go and move on to the next
Don't waste any time pretending to grieve

You had your fun, we shared some time
It was nice while it lasted, no ties
Disposable like the papers you read
Totally honest, not laden with lies

Lindsay Sinclair, Bristol, Avon

SNOWFLAKES

One delicate, pristine snowflake floated gently down
Alighting on the intense cold of a rusty rail
Then another, then another

Until the rust of the rail was completely obliterated
Soon a white wall of wonder was covering everything
For as far as the eye could see

Still the snow fell thick and fast, a white curtain of lace
As gentle as a feather's touch and as soft as duckdown
Each with its own pattern

Each a tiny sculpture, never to be copied
Then gone in an instant with the blinking of the sun

Dora Watkins, Bridgwater, Somerset

FRIENDS

If actions speak louder than words,
Over the years,
Yours were shouting from the rooftops.

If portraits were painted with words,
My life would be a gallery,
Illustrated with your kindness.

If laughter was a currency,
I would be rich,
Beyond my wildest dreams.

Wendy Paddick, Glastonbury, Somerset

ALTAR EGO

How soft the tender moon
with love's romantic touch,
how strong its gentle light,
inspires the giving heart -

Then, in an instant,
no thunder warning -

the brash and searing sun
usurps, engulfs the mood;
its venom-brightness reigns,
to shadows drives that heart:

the moon cries, *Mercy*,
from sun's hot ego -

but heat burns harsher still,
exerts its self-led will,
so love chills sad as ice
now moon's made sacrifice.

Martin Perry, Bristol, Avon

87

FORM

There are rules of course,
Although now it is forbidden to list them.
You must allude to things
Sidelong.
Like a cat in long grass,
Never name a thing directly,
For by naming it, it loses its power.

In another country, by the cherry blossom,
Friends would sit each spring,
Batting Haiku.
How delicate, how subtle,
To squeeze so much into so little,
Saying more by what is left out.

We don't have rules now
And things fall apart.

Making pretty shapes as they drift
on the wind.

Peter Prochazka, Bristol, Avon

WALKING THE PIERS

Now, when each slope's a hill,
all pebbles boulders,
we walk arms linked,
one pacing the other,
the pier our level meeting ground.
Like fisher wives awaiting the catch
we lean into the wind,
folding against icy blasts.

Once the captain of beach expeditions,
laden with buckets, baskets, spades,
you guided us all over cliff and rock-fall,
counted our heads in the waves.

Back in the car, the years slip from you
as you watch a red sail board
in the hands of a dancer,
skim and swoop, jumping waves
with the liquid grace of a young girl.
You breathe the rhythm,
following in and out,
your face shining with spray.

Jo Phillips, Langport, Somerset

PORLOCK

A day, deep in January.
Heavy, grey sky,
Unreflective, unrelieved.

Yet here, under skeletal trees
Where the stream widens,
Clear water reveals stone and shale,
Rich in the muted golds and browns
Of an English autumn,

Recalling friendlier days.

Rosemary Toeman, Porlock, Somerset

WILD

This feeling smells like a forest;
damp, musky, rich, clear
and a deer sniffing the air
ready to run.
This feeling sounds like the snap of a twig
somewhere in the distance.
This feeling lives in the wild places,
far away, hard to reach,
unknown territory.
This feeling is hiding, but not well enough.
It is creeping up, stalking me.
It is almost ready to pounce.

Jo Waterworth, Glastonbury, Somerset

LISTEN

Strange twilight hours
Now silently falling
All things have gone home
The whole world at peace
Deep in the woodlands
A dark bird calling,
Then nearer and nearer
The wings of wild geese
Beating in from the sea,
Where a wild wind is sending
Them over the clifftops,
As higher they soar.
So be quiet and listen,
As daylight is ending
To the music around you
When all sounds are blending
Waves in the white trees
Wild wings on the shore.

Peggy Cooper, Highworth, Wiltshire

TIME PASSING

October afternoon. I sit,
on a broken seat, rotten with damp,
listening to the leaves fall.
Rust glazes a distant row of beech.
The heavy quiet is scratched by a crow's call
and daisy rays of light
are scored by a crow's flight.
Spattered starlings speckle
the watercolour sky.
I sit, on my crumbling bench,
watching time go by.
Listening to the leaves fall.

Gill Minter, Chippenham, Wiltshire

THE JACKDAW

Menacing blue eyes
Swaggering, strutting bully
In black livery.

Stentorian screech
Repelling all marauders,
Threatening posture.

Top drawer hooligan,
I would give you an ASBO,
If only I could.

Hostile invader,
In to my garden you fly,
Jackdaw, Nemesis.

Kathy Wilson, Devizes, Wiltshire

92

East
Anglia

WAS IT A LEAP YEAR?

Her strict upbringing and high class
Did forbid any kind of courting,
Nonetheless, she madly fell in love
At twenty.

Adoring and idolising her fiance.
To her, it seemed all the birds
Were singing in happiness.
The world was not the same from then,
She was the boss, but also a slave
Of that love.

Still, protocol had to be followed;
Rules are rules, no one can change them,
Or, was it someone's imagination?
There are no barriers
That love cannot cross, and
A way was found to put an end to it all.

Was it a leap year?
I do not know, I wasn't there.
But, it is said that she asked him,
Albert, will you marry me?

Victoria E Tejedor, Cambridge, Cambridgeshire

UPLANDER

Wet grass bestows the scented air
With springtime's tune,
Of birdsong fair,
For wading through the lawns of June
Our blackbird sifts without due care,
For lunch amidst fresh cuttings strewn.

Thin fronds of old man's beard drift by,
Settling down
And dancing high,
They raise ten smiles for every frown
As each enraptures, mystifies,
With childish whimsy like a clown.

To rise above the flooded fen
Reminds me of,
Those times since when,
The wake of heron from above
Whose ripples, now erased by men,
Should grace these waters I now love.

Asa Humphreys, Ely, Cambridgeshire

SILENCE

Sometimes,
in silence you speak;
words unheard,
unseen, yet
reaching out,
touching the depths;
silently
shedding light,
maybe just a glimmer,
In the darkness.

Sometimes,
you spell it out
so clearly,
yet I fail
to see the obvious;
your patience
astounds me,
I've missed it again,
yet you're there still,
in the silence.

Lindy Jane Rainbow, Ely, Cambridgeshire

ATTILA THE INVIGILATOR

Attila the Invigilator roars in like fury
From the dark plains of the east.
He is furnace and slaughter.
Not for him the spice roads,
The silken girls of Samarkand;
He is storm and darkness
And white fire also.
The desert unlocks in his throat,
The primeval places, the mountain
Of initiation. Before you know it
He snares you with his fission eye,
A glint of gold teeth.
His thighs flow with liquid music,
He quivers like an animal.

O Attila, Prince of Invigilators,
Examine me!
I've done my revision,
I'll not be found wanting,
Just test me out ...
Come on in, hun!

Rex Collinson, Cottenham, Cambridgeshire

SILENT WHISPERINGS

Solitary, yet crowded
Pale gravestones in the midst
Hunched
Smooth pebbles
Bend on water-sodden soil
The sea drained out of it
My son's eyes grow larger
As he caresses the drowning mud
With his little giving hands
Pigeon spied in the distance
Entombed in silent whisperings

Kathryn Aybak, Cottenham, Cambridgeshire

EARTH'S TIME

The earth here lies awaiting
The trumpet call of spring,
So desolate, so cold, so bare,
Her sombre winter coat.

The streams lie still and silent,
They hide 'neath opaque glass.
Yet death will soon now flee away,
New life will sound her note

For all creation, hidden,
To rise and bloom once more.
The seed, here dead, must live again,
To pour forth colours bright

Through rays of sun, now warming,
Doth still great mystery hold,
To bring the bough to perfect life,
This awe-inspiring sight.

Derek Lane, Peterborough, Cambridgeshire

NEW ORLEANS

Orange blossom scent invades latin quarter.
Sleeping residents wake with night stranger,
Midnight lover, dawn alien, cigar-stale lace curtains, frail
from constancy of tugging hands.
Balcony leans, woman stands, wipes her sweating memory
of whisky-sour breath whispers away, breathing in the
scented day.
Cotton bales, swell in their queue,
Hard bitten hands hook them to the bay.
Mississippi gambler, too drunk to feel the sway, throws
silver dollar down to dancing children, midst their dusty
play.
Gambling tables wait for *lady luck*, to bring dismay.
Temperance ladies, bustles high, pass by, frowning,
Doom is nigh.
Glancing at the figure, on reputed balcony,
Never speak to her, be their religious philosophy.
Paddle steamboat coughs goodbye, sweetheart wipes a
tearful eye.
Gambler vanishes from sight, living out his endless night,
fortune farther out of sight.
Woman turns back to the room of man's dark soul's
twilight, brushes hair, dons ruffled dresses, to vanish
forever, into the night.

Betty Fenton, Hunstanton, Norfolk

YESTERDAY'S CHILDREN

Oh, where have they gone, all those years that have flown?
So quickly they've passed, now the children have grown.
Just an album of snapshots, tucked away in a drawer,
Is all that is left of the days gone before.

But we look at them sometimes and turn back the clock,
To the time when we had our own babies to rock.
To the days when our children just played in the sun,
When tricycles, mud pies and puddles were fun.

Yesterday's children, that faraway age,
They're here once again, smiling up from the page.
Play days and school days, too quickly they've flown.
For our children now have homes of their own.

There are grandchildren too, and to me it seems plain,
Those faraway times, well they do come again.
When tricycles, mud pies and puddles are fun,
For I still have children who play in the sun.

Sylvia Waller, Norwich, Norfolk

THE DISCHARGED SAILORS' AND SOLDIERS' ALLOTMENTS

He straightens up stiffly, a cough barks out,
Howitzer-like and he takes the recoil stoically.
He slowly stares at the rows of turned earth
And pensively pauses his chin on the slimed rake's end.
And now his mind's eye sees a far-off earth,
A flooded lowland, a thick soup of wet mud, viscous.
Boots and puttees soaked, strangling his numb calves,
Caped and huddled against the ruthless, relentless rain.
He hears the cough and the thud of distant guns
And waits, poised and tensed to feel the shrapnell's tearings,
For the cries and the moans, the limbs torn off,
The chests and bellies shredded by shards of shell casing,
Of faces so well known. The cheeky grins,
Chuckles that never fade, even after all these years.
He stoops again, back bent to the dark earth
And smoothes and settles the shy sodden clods, lovingly.

John Roebuck, Holt, Norfolk

WHEN IN PINK MY TREE IS DRESSED

When in pink my tree is dressed,
Sweet nature's breath it courts,
Fleeting joy and innocence,
Embodied in their waltz.

Framed by heaven's golden eye,
In passing nature's gift,
Only but two moons before
Such beauty ne'er exist.

In wrinkled sorrow, brown and bare,
None did my tree embrace,
But bitter frost and morning mist
And time's eternal race.

Sepia though my memories be,
This I know of my sweet tree;
Life's great journey holds more worth
Than passing beauty and rush'd mirth.

Charmaine Dunsmore, Kenninghall, Norfolk

WILL SHE SEE?

What can I do to win your heart back,
To have your love to take?

What can I do, but look at you and realise,
I never had it in the first place.

Your fake smile,
I'm crawling to catch her beautiful tears.
I fear she doesn't see me,
Maybe one day she will.

Ben Harrison, Great Yarmouth, Norfolk

AUTUMN GLORY

Autumn arrives and nature's colours change
To red and gold, as if the fading sun,
Sensing the imminence of waning strength,
Pours out his all in one last glorious burst
Of radiance and heat.
Harvest is in and orchards yield their store.
Blackberries shine in hedgerows
And baskets filled, jam makers rejoice.
Rose hips and haws, like glow-worms, light the lanes,
A treasure trove for birds.
Children run laughing through the fallen leaves,
Squirrels find nuts for their future store.
The wood smoke hangs in cooling air,
Reminding us that winter soon will bring
The year's perfected course.

Jane Dorling, Diss, Norfolk

MARCH OF PROGRESS

Is it here I walked in younger days?
Hearing wind in the trees,
Feeling hot, golden rays,
Is it here that I walked in my youth?

Is it here that I walked in younger days?
Where soft-eyed cattle cropped lush green grass
And a dragonfly floated gently past,
Is it here that I walked in my youth?

Is it here that I walked in younger days?
Is it here, amid the new city's haze?
Where people hurry with vacant gaze,
Is it here that I walked in my youth?

Marilyn Lyne, Ipswich, Suffolk

MIXED EMOTIONS

Summer dresses, Sunday picnics,
Mother's smiles and sunshine.
Her oppression, my depression,
Her isolation and mine.

Shafts of sunbeams glancing
Through the woodland walks,
Down wild flower ways.
With such fondness I remember
All those hazy summer days.

Times of tension, fear and sorrow,
Bewildered, frightened over the years
And just like the weeping willow,
How I drooped and shed my tears.

Pamela Garrod, Lowestoft, Suffolk

WE ARE BOTH HIS OTHER WOMAN

I am not the other woman
She is not the wife who fails to understand him
I am not his secret mistress
She is not the most important part of his life
I am his English passion
She is his Irish public wife

I am his only soulmate, she is his only rock
I am his dream, she is his security
I am his sexual ecstasy
She is his comfort zone
I am his spiritual partner
She is his family roots
I am his challenge
She is his safety
I am all that he ever dreamed of
She is the history he cannot leave behind
I am his greatest love and his greatest fear
She is his routine and his even keel

I am the one and only love of his life
She is his mediocre, but easy life

Sarah Caddick, Felixstowe, Suffolk

HOW OLD ARE WE?

Age is but a number.
Aeons of precious seconds tick by
As we live out our complex lives.
Our minds harbour copious moods and feelings
And our recollection is tested daily.
How little we know,
How little we understand.
They say the sky is our limit of knowledge,
The apparent vault of heaven
Is our aim.
When?
No one knows,
Let's just live and enjoy.

Carol Shipley, Beccles, Suffolk

ON THE BUST OF LEWIS WILLIAMS IN UNIVERSITY LIBRARY, CARDIFF

Balefully, glaring eyes gaze spacefully
Thinking of youth, dreaming
Perhaps of alcoves of time,
Wandering, wondering lost.

Black-browed carbonate creature
Is all well with thee, old man?
Or are you cursing the coursers
Of time who haunt your memory?

Life is fast slipping through the sieve
Of time, only strained symbols of dusty death
Remember to taunt you and teach you of life.
Where you ever young? Life in
Death has treated you well old man
Dumbly listening to our whisp'ring visions

Grahame Tanner, Ipswich, Suffolk

East
Midlands

I USED TO BE

I used to be someone's baby,
They wiped away my tears.
I used to be someone's daughter,
But not for many years.
I used to be someone's mummy
And I dispelled all their fears.

I used to make decisions,
Advise people what to do.
I used to plan my future,
Also see it through.
I am now that silly old lass,
She can't remember yesterday,
Only her long lost past.

Christine Garner, Chesterfield, Derbyshire

MMM

Modern day Atlantis, lost beneath the flood
Marie Celeste Atlantians gone
Mud covering their tiled floors
Mist at dawn, clouding their world

Many generations of habitation
Murky beneath the aquatic shroud
Mankind's unwelcome legacy
Mighty in its destruction

Messengers of doom ignored
Money silencing their wisdom
Mistakes always denied
Misunderstanding the alleged reason

Stuart Bunting, Chaddesden, Derbyshire

A WRITER'S WORLD

On a rainy day, the sun beams through
While rain patters, the sun shines
As clouds turn grey, they fade away
To reveal the world's greatest finds

A tear of sadness, is a drop of joy
A terror scream, is a burst of laughter
A broken heart is the beginning
Of a new happily every after

Reality and imagination
Come together to make one world
In a writer's mind, both are combined
And no stone is left unturned

Imagination unlocks every door
A string of words can mean so much
Anything is possible
For as long as pen and paper touch

aDele Morgan, Derby, Derbyshire

IT'S A NEW DAY

I will stop making excuses
for all my pain,
I will ignore my losses
and count my gains.

I will not postpone
my joy or wait
for someday.
Today is a new day,
I choose to make it
the very best day.

Shilla Mutamba, Coalville, Leicestershire

NIGHTDRESS

The day puts on an evening gown
In shades of softest night
Wearing a crown of diamond stars
That glitter clear and bright
The moon, a brooch of lustrous pearl
Festooned in silver chains of cloud
Looks down upon a silent world
That's patient but unbowed
Sowing a crop of seed-pearl snow
Dainty soft and white
A wind of satin scatters them
Reflecting all stray light
On silent feet in ice-silk slippers
Dancing gaily down the marbled streams
Gliding over forests of sun worshippers
Now wrapped up tight in white-velvet dreams

Robert Palmer-Wilson, Leicester, Leicestershire

FANFARE

Blood red,
Bleeding -
The field of Flanders' spew,
In the wind the poppy heads blowing
Salute the dying man.

Just a boy,
His youth manifests
The love his eyes disguise,
As slow the sunset settles
Over painful, captured land.

Red lips,
Soon to be moving,
A name his heart desired,
His mother, lover, companion,
Steals the death defining time.

Gorged lashes,
Closing -
Sweeping low the pallid cheeks,
As into the realms of eternity
The man of war will creep.

Mo Ward, Hinckley, Leicestershire

AFTER THE FLOOD

Then the rain came, giant droplets hit me hard
Repelled, I curled in a ball, seeing out the violent squall.

After the rain
The air felt alive
Fresh with an expectation
Like an electrical charge
And slowly I uncurled
The sun lifting each limb
Like the first crocus that broke
On the brick burnt land.

First light and first hope
Produces a swathe of colour
Dancing incandescent and bright
On a gathering breeze
In time, a whole ecosystem is born
Sustained it will grow on
Did I create this? Or was it wrought
Out of such intolerable hurt?

Then the rains come, and they never stop
Until everything is lost.

Rob Adams, Anstey, Leicestershire

AT THE END OF A TROPICAL STORM

Bulbul in the mimosa tree
Rejoices in the rain
Calls to a mynah down below
Who sings to a different strain

Droplets fall from leaf to leaf
Like crystals from a cord
They sparkle in the evening light
Gems from a sultan's hoard

The waxen lotus bends her head
Each leaf clasps a jewel
Bats dip down to sip from them
Like nectar, sweet and cool

Deep within the plashy pond
The frogs begin to call
The storm has faded out to sea
And peace reigns over all

Julia Knight, Louth, Lincolnshire

POOR PEOPLE

The ill
come to me,
and I touch
their worried brow,
and give them
strength,
power,
faith,
an aspirin
and elastoplast,
and they think
I'm God.

G Merritt, Hardingstone, Northamptonshire

IMAGERY

My pen is propelled by personal pleasure
And is no competition for nature;
The changing landscape interrupts my thoughts.
The sun flirts with each of the passing clouds,
At times she dismisses them all en masse
And parades alone. Her golden glory
Sending a glowing vista beneath her,
Commanding the shadows to shrink or stretch.
A medley of colours match and mingle,
Meandering to distant fading shades,
Culminating to a blue-green marriage.
Two universes touching, yet worlds apart,
More powerful than my pondering pen;
My pen that tries to portray the image,
The image that nature has created.

June Ayling, Weedon Bec, Northamptonshire

SURFING RHAPSODIE

Grey, dark and light
Raging, fierce waves,
Smash, crush to smithereens
Of sharp, dazzling white.

Men, courageous and sinewy
Twisted bodies in pirouettes spinning,
Trying to catch their dream
In flight with surfing rhapsodie.

Waves, but in the sky,
Souls, play laugh and fly,
Fall freely down,
Never to crash or to die.

Black, navy, white,
Why? - They will never reply.

Nadine Platt, Wellingborough, Northamptonshire

BROKEN TRUST

No trust is more foolish than of the faith
Placed in the hands of one's fellow man,
For more than mere confidence lays at stake
When hope becomes the magician's
Cunning slight of hand.
Subjected to the scrutiny of the luminous reality,
Beliefs will always fade
As the sun-paled words upon the printed page,
Relating to the folly that is humanity,
The hidden savagery of a naked ape.
Delude yourself not with matters of consideration;
Ask no favour and none will be asked of you,
For each rogue looks for guileless saviour
To nail each sin into mortal sinew.

William Shaun Milligan, Corby, Northamptonshire

DUST IN THE SUNLIGHT FLOATS

Sunshine streamed into the corner of the room
where the dust settled into jagged silence.

Although the wall was cracked, the rust sprang
away from the debris that hung thick in splayed
painful circles.

She sat in the pungent sulphur, cleaning the place
where the washstand had lain broken for three weeks.

The green of the slatted window frame teased the
bluebottle, that feasted on the mellow toffee.

And she knew the greenhouse was full of butterflies.

Sally Keeling, Towcester, Northamptonshire

WALKING IN MITERDALE

If nobody told you,
You wouldn't know it was there;
A secret valley,
Away from the madding crowd.
A lane almost hidden by ferny fronds,
To a parking place within Ireby Forest.
Walking boots on, dogs at the ready,
Follow the beck as it runs across rocks,
Up the valley, keeping close to the beck.
A desolate place, not a soul to be seen
Except the Herdwick's grazing grass that's barely green.
The Miter's journey is only beginning
From a rock on a hillside,
Water gurgling up from deep within.
Our journey carries on to Burnmoor Tarn
To an old shooting lodge, which is now just a barn,
Through the swirling mist we can see Great Gable.
A formidable task, for those that are able,
Solitude is a wondrous pleasure,
Take time out and enjoy its treasures.

Isobel Burks, Kettering, Northamptonshire

ANTITHESIS IN THE ARBORETUM

Cheek on the sward, sun on my thigh,
Sight-seeing nature with an all-seeing eye.
Babel of birds, breasts swollen with pride,
Feeding their young, then strutting aside,
Keeping one eye out for innocent me,
The other for the sweep of death, down from a tree.

Remembering the sorrow, recalling the pain
Of a tangle of feathers, red-tipped in the rain.

Then skimming the grass, skipping in haste,
I saw two thrushes, one chasing, one chaste.
Intent on escape, yet not deigning to fly,
Risking its virtue, forsaking the sky.
Foolish bird, take wing, arise,
Foolish me, so unworldly, unwise.

Cheek on the sward, sun on my thigh,
Procreation and death in the blink of an eye.

Bill Hawley, Nottingham, Nottinghamshire

SKYLARK

A skylark flies up from the stubble
with liquid notes bubbling from its throat.
It rises higher, with wings shivering,
mouth open, throat quivering,
at the effort of producing such joyous notes.

Still ascending, the lark's song seems unending,
as each note blends one into the next,
until its warbling and trilling,
overflows and begins filling
the air around with pure refreshing sound.

Yet, even though the lark is soaring,
it continues pouring out its vibrant song.
Until, at the zenith of its flight
and set, in silhouette, against the light,
I just sit and watch and listen with delight.

And yet, I wonder,
does the lark send salutations to the sun?
Or is it joie de vivre, sheer exuberance and fun?

George Shipley, Mansfield Woodhouse, Nottinghamshire

A LIFETIME AGO

There is a look that reflects a lifetime
Of dreams and might have beens.

There is a kiss that promises tomorrow,
But marks yesterday with blissful reminiscence
Of a shadowy dream from long ago.

Of a time when we could have made reality into what?

We can never know.

Laughter in your eyes still has a youthful gleam,
A look that echoes the past, yet promises the future.

I see beyond the years,
To a boy who became a man,

And yet,
However brief,

History binds us,
As only shared history can.

                                    Cheryl Ward, Newark, Nottinghamshire

West Midlands

DARKLY DREAMING

We all hide something
Inside
Another part, a secret self
Dark-half of our souls

However innocent they look
Inside
There's always something
Secret thoughts, serial killers

Be good, stay in control
Inside
Never letting out
That shadow side

For most the whispers
Inside
Can be ignored, but for me
I hear them screaming
I know they're scheming
The voices are multiplying, are teeming
Inside
As I lie here darkly dreaming

Laura Meryl Ross, Hereford, Herefordshire

A NEW DAWN

The iron railing stands
Strong and firm before the door.
And in between the posts
The spider's web with minute droplets
Waves gently in the breeze.
Circles of beads, round and round,
Glisten in the new day's sun.

Jenny Renowden, Wythall, Worcestershire

DIFFERENT

The boys
Saw a white blackbird

There he sat
Improbable as a unicorn
Solid as a potato
Real as love -
Singing.

Because he was different
The boys
Grew very excited
Because he was different
The boys
Stoned him to death.

Tom Freeman-Keel, Craven Arms, Shropshire

THE WINTER OAK

The thaw freezes in the late afternoon.

The sun drifts lower in the western sky.
Ice candles flicker in refracted light,
Twisting candelabra intertwining
Through the branches, riven bark defining.
Tight knots badge the trunk, whirls of moss cocoon,
Deep weathered grooves like some Druidic rune,
Inspiring remnants of some ancient rite.
Angled hoar frost twigs, intercrossing white
Stretch upwards in a latticed canopy,
Trapping the outline of the nimbus moon.

Pearl berries, dropped from sickled mistletoe,
Lie scattered on paw-pitted snow below
And pecked at by a curious passing crow.

Wood pigeons flap by in slow-bellied flight,
The roosting scrimmage will be starting soon,
Dislodging flakes of snow along the bough.
A vixen's cry splinters approaching night,
Shadows lengthen, merging in sepia tones.

The thaw freezes in the late afternoon.

Don Nixon, Albrighton, Shropshire

ONLY A THOUGHT

All that rises
Out of the ground
Must return,
Whether the wild rose
Or the buildings of man.

Leaf-dust, coal-dust,
Is there no difference
In the end?
No distinction
In the dark earth?

Only the new flower
Is pure and separate,
Though the bright petal
Contains the form
Of its fading.

And in our dancing
We are already still,
Our echoing laughter
Contains the sound
Of future silence.

Dorothy Buyers, Oswestry, Shropshire

FIELD SCENE

Peace is brought by the grass
that feeds the lazy cows and sheep
as they idle amongst their enclosure.

Broken up by dry stone walls
that meander randomly,
following the earth's contours.

The pile of rubble now almost matches
the size of the abandoned barn
from whence it came.

Only the trees swaying in the wind
add movement to
this still beauty.

In the warmer weather
walkers will visit nearby,
but for now they leave this pasture undisturbed.

This tranquil beauty remains untouched
and will do so
for another hundred years.

Sam Chater, Leek, Staffordshire

MOONLIGHTING

Once upon a cloudless night sky,
We lovers love, then lie and sigh.
I see reflected in your eye,
Silver lunar satellite,
Comet tails and stars so bright,
In slow eclipse as sleep steals by,
I hold my breath and watch all night.

Phillip Jupp, Uttoxeter, Staffordshire

MONKS

The monk said he wanted
To tell me a secret,
But then he remembered,
His vow of silence.

Leonard Cohen had
Been a monk,
But then he remembered
A room in the Chelsea Hotel;
A former life,
And left.

I never knew the monk's secret,
I just knew his silence,
But that silence
Spoke volumes.

Ben Mcnair, Lichfield, Staffordshire

THIS WOMAN

Striking red blood on the tips of her fingers,
Shocking pink rose petals causing her lips to blush,
Drops of the ocean in her eyes.
Powerful.
To men, this woman is at her worst.
Tattered satin only just draping over her shoulders,
A four-inch lift on her feet from the cobbled alleyway about
to snap,
Uncontrollable laughter emerging from her mouth.
Defenceless.
To men, this woman is at her best.
Nowhere to turn,
No longer any energy,
No more sense,
No more respect for herself,
To men, this woman is now perfect.

Laura Challinor, Stoke-on-Trent, Staffordshire

INDUSTRY GHOSTS

Walking in the park we fell
Deeply into each other's eyes,
Drowning under blackest seas.
An opaque frost tranced the air,
Hard as diamond,
Filigree on fragile leaf.
Our breath coiled like white serpents
And cold fingers clutched for warmth
Through the park watched the brick houses
And ghosts of bottle kilns no longer there,
Absence of shadows against the skyline.
The potteries lay in jewelled antiquity,
The pulse now within the retailed glass,
The glacial roads white as fine bone china.
Walking in the park you took my hand
And the ghosts dreamed on,
Their tears turning to ice as my heart melted.

Lisa Pallin, Stoke-on-Trent, Staffordshire

THE CLOWN

Bring on the clown,
the one with the black painted, teardrop
stark,
against so white a face.
So we can shed tears of merriment
as he struts,
falls and tumbles
with unfailing grace.
A livid, scarlet gash
of grinning,
sorrow cannot erase.
A medley of clashing colour,
the garish garb of patches, wilted flowers
our eyes, with greed feast on.

A sudden sidelong glance reveals
two smouldering, long, dead coals.
No firelight in those orbs,
Warmth, is there none
as glaring at the company
he bows
and then is gone.

Shirley Wood, Stafford, Staffordshire

AUTUMN

The middle years of caring
Are the middle years of sharing
Half-forgotten dreams of early loving
Of pausing to recall the laughter, tears and all
The pride that filled
The busy years
Yet still the echoes sound
With voices all around
The laughing, singing young ones
And the old ones gently fading into quiet
Now the loving down the years
That mingled with the tears
Has grown into a tender bond, so strong
That all the cares and fears
Which fill the middle years
Are as the leaves that fall
In autumn time

Jean White, Warwick, Warwickshire

THUNDEROUS

Black thunder sky
Left corner of my eye

Visualised

Heavy with the swell
Multiplied evaporation
Awaiting moment to dispel

Eject the torrent
Hailstone bounce

Announced

Arrival of cooler climate
Of forceful air

Droplets forming a forewarning
Injects fresh notes

Conquering the stillness

Laura Smith, Bulkington, Warwickshire

THE RICH MAN IN HIS CASTLE, THE POOR MAN AT HIS GATE

The high-class lady sewing, the low-class making chain,
The both of them are yearning, to relieve their weight of pain.
The Madam from her Master, the Mistress from her work,
The lives of each - disaster, alike as cheese from chalk.
The two of them are equal, in everything but worth.
Though Ma'ams riches are her Master's, the Mistresses' her Beau's,
The each of them want freedom, they're prisoners of their fate.
They each await their kingdom, in hovel and estate.
Who has the greatest freedom? The Mistress? The Madam?
Making chain or sewing, living lustily or calm?
Each longs for something different, as is the wont of man.

The grass, it grows the greenest, when it's just out of reach,
So, hard luck you sweet ladies; that's what the menfolk teach.

Peter Sammons, Rugby, Warwickshire

A DEPARTURE

Heart full of grief,
eyes suffused with tears.
He decided a last wander brief
in his neighbourhood spheres.
His popular places appealed to his final close inspection,
to him now they are beyond comparison.
At home there was a great hush,
relatives and friends in did rush,
feeling their hearts to swell
to bid him farewell.
Calm and unmoved stood the fellow,
but we all know
he must had felt deep sorrow.

J Grizzell, Wolverhampton, West Midlands

LUST

Man yearns, he longs for things that cannot be,
Pursuing goals beyond his wildest grasp
And reaches into realms of fantasy,
For short, ecstatic times which cannot last.
This manifested greed, his passion raw,
Led onwards by his weak and shallow thought
Is just ephemeral longing, nothing more,
A hasty taste of pleasure he has sought.
Much better than to value other treasure,
Feel thankful for the fellowship of friends,
For wisdom, faith and joy in utmost measure,
Uncompromising love that has no end.
Be gone. These thoughts of envy, greed and lust,
They can't compare with true and steadfast trust.

Margaret Worsley, Coventry, West Midlands

MIDNIGHT DANCE OF THE STARS

You the stars that danced so
gracefully under the moonlight gaze,
Relished an enchanted
and enthralling phase.
The snowy owl perched dignified
on the wise oak tree,
Wished to shimmer so magically
upon the sapphire sky and be so free.

The silver illuminated ripples
on the crystal-eyed sea,
Boisterously mirrored the magnificent midnight dance
progressing to be part of thee.
Yet you lustrous liberal stars
roam the sleeping heavens near and afar.
Your dancing, radiant by your light,
Until dawn's kiss, wishing you goodnight.

Aradhna Jaswal, Bilston, West Midlands

LARGO

First, let the trail go stone cold
Pack the bloodhounds off to bed
Put all urgent calls on hold
Deal the cards, black and red

Let the evidence go astray
Feed the news-hounds what they crave
Watch the witnesses walk away
Titbits for tomorrows save

Footprints fade with turn of season
Though the foxhounds scent their prey
Notebooks stored, without good reason?
No, they will see the light of day

When placemen, checking dusty diaries
Fearing wolfhounds at the gate
Announce at last delayed enquiries
And leave the scapegoat to his fate

Jack Kerr, Coventry, West Midlands

THE GRACE OF LOVE

You are the keeper of my secrets,
My lover, my friend, my witness.
We have travelled a lifetime together,
Across capricious weather of distant lands
That tore at our hearts and tore at our hands,
Seeking to burn love where it stands.
We've seen our horizons rimmed with fire
And could not escape the biting ice,
But nothing could crush the healing desire
To see our love through to the other side.
And faith was rewarded with this blessed place
That we wander in now, with joy unbound,
The gardens we have found are infused with grace,
Born from our love are these hallowed grounds.
We held to hope and trust, and now we can see,
These gifts, when bound with love, are alchemy.
So the love that binds a husband and wife,
Transcends to soul communion,
That lives on beyond life.

Mahmuda Chowdhury, Birmingham, West Midlands

DREAMS OF SEEDS

I dreamt dreams of seeds
Seeds that shun living water
Seeds that give bright colours
To all persons in their shoal
And transform them into lovely babies

I love to scatter seeds
In every patch of valuable ground
Starting here to that volatile corner
This surface journey seems heavier
Than the might to advance with the adventure

I see blood dripping in every global part
Its sight being a relish to men
The pain that follows blood is sweet wine
That hardens men's hearts to steel
And creates a turbulence of destructive forces

God, may you give me absolute power
To scatter my binding seeds endlessly
Seeds that give birth to serene hearts
Hearts that are full of love and piety
My dream seeds of eternal peace and abundant love

Kenneth Nengovhela, Wolverhampton, West Midlands

North West

A VILLANELLE FOR DAYBREAK

The dappled sky presents another morn,
a gift of wonder, one of nature's best.
There is no day that passes without dawn.

The show begins with curtains widely drawn,
once gentle folks have risen from their rest.
The dappled sky presents another morn.

Occurring since the earth was newly born,
when Adam romped with Eve in Eden's nest.
There is no day that passes without dawn.

A yellow eye encourages the corn,
its journey blazing high from east to west.
The dappled sky presents another morn.

Unbroken blue or grey skies, rent and torn,
provide for us a daily weather test.
There is no day that passes without dawn.

Though repetition often causes scorn,
the daybreak is exempt and truly blessed.
The dappled sky presents another morn.
There is no day that passes without dawn.

Gay Horton, Macclesfield, Cheshire

THE RAIN

The rain falls
And I sit in the car alone.
Seeing couples hand in hand
In love.
And I cry, but that's okay
No one can see because it's raining.
I can sit here and watch life unfold
The cafés, shops and bars
Exciting places to go
For others.
I can't even imagine us together like this
Hand in hand.
No time or energy to spare, ever
Not for a snatched moment or long-awaited surprise
Nothing to dress up for, look forward to.
So we have the same old grind,
Years and years and years.
Love has grown tired and nothing is new.

Christine Rowley, Winterley, Cheshire

MAGNIFICAT

Your rays sear in on a million
Steamy motes
Gilding my body with gold and
Embracing my nakedness
With mid-May's warmth
As I step from the shower in my
Birthday suit.

And I think of my mother,
Her pain,
As she laboured for me
Upon this day
All those years ago ...
In a rare Birmingham heatwave.

Would that explain my inordinate
Desire for the sun's kiss?

Meg Marsden, Poynton, Cheshire

A NEW DAY BECKONS

I watch darkness envelop the earth
See it stop my life in the fast lane,
hear silence as tree branches
solidify in the night air; shredding my senses.

I smell the cold, touch the frozen bark.
Lean against stone slabs,
stand with the stillness of a photograph.
Then I curl up. Sleep.

Sun's warmth wakens,
I feel her rays loosen me.
Smell the new dawn. Hear waking
birds, barking dogs, smell toast.

I am me again. My life
returns as the sky is painted gold.
I hear the new day beckon.
It calls persistently.

I am free, my limbs light.
The memories which climbed my throat
are gone. I am ready for whatever
this new day has in store.

Dorothea Carroll, Chester, Cheshire

EVERY VIOLIN

The wind still blows in from the shore
Your rhythm flows across my face
I see the waves that formed an open door
Alas, of you, there is no trace
You didn't see me frown
When I learned your plane went down
I felt numb and couldn't feel
And thinking, *Is this real?*
I always loved you from the start
You were the owner of my heart
Your strings of love and joy and care
You gave to me, for us to share
It's been a year since September
It's time to think, to remember
I remember all the love you gave
And memories for me to save
You touched my soul from deep within
Your orchestra plays inside my heart
And I will always hear
Every violin

Joshua Brian De Vere, Frodsham, Cheshire

THE OLD HANDBAG

They found the old handbag in a drawer,
It had lain there for years.
Its contents told us all her story,
Her highs, lows, joys and fears.

The watch that stopped many years ago
Was a birthday present.
Paper clips were left from office days,
Days she grew to resent.

The notebook held her scribbled poems,
Now for the world to see.
That half-crown was from a special year,
Perhaps that held the key.

At the bottom, a shopping receipt,
A lipstick, still bright pink,
The handbag, very old and battered
Told more than you might think.

Angela Pritchard, Sandbach, Cheshire

THE FULMAR

The fulmar feeds and flies in the gale's bitter teeth
Strong winds chill the bones, this land of saints and tides.
In the island church, prayers for the dead and dying
Memory imprinted in the genetic blueprint of a people.
Not the saint's imprint but the unsanctified
Across hostile waters that will win in the end
Swamp these lands and wash out the memory,
Unsettle the settlements and turn the village to raw
Earth, sand dunes. Scatter the sheep, unfold the lambs.
Listen carefully to the caterwauling wind
This thin place between heaven and earth
This place of quiet death, of wailing birth.

Geoffrey Smith, Carlisle, Cumbria

MUSIC FOR AN AUDIENCE

A bang, a crash, the shaking of peas,
Keep in time with the rhythm please,
A keyboard, some flutes, and a big oboe;
Make a noise and let the music flow.
Some guitars, a fiddle and a cello join in
Make beautiful music, to some - for others, a din.
Music brings young and old together,
To share a concert and express whatever.
The emotions and moods the composers did pen,
Music looks back and into the future -
Its influence is universal, even way back when.
So put on your best frock,
Have a break from heavy rock,
Classical can be powerful and upbeat;
So hurry please and take your seat.

Linda Dixon, Workington, Cumbria

MY GUILTY PLEASURE

We all have shameless cravings,
some more so than others.
Either flaunting them out in the open
or keeping them under the covers.

If my own guilty pleasure merits
a spell in Her Majesty's jail,
then the Eurovision Song Contest
is my prime suspect, without fail.

I've heard brilliant songs and awful songs,
I've seen many a crime against fashion.
Even lousy-cum-cheesy choreography
has never dimmed my Euro passion.

In my twenty one years as a Euro fan,
I've watched many paupers and knaves.
But for me, the Queen of Eurovision
will always be Katrina (and the Waves).

For my love of the contest, I get stick.
But I dismiss it all with my *sang froid*.
Because, one day, I'll hear the legend again
That is - Le Royaume Uni, douze points.

John Hastings, Workington, Cumbria

THE FATE OF MAN

Out of the darkness came a light
A light so bright it shone for the right
The sword of justice was its name
And no-one knew from whence it came

And the grim reaper held its blade
A time for taking stock and weeding out the chafe
And to start looking upon man's fate
Because now for man it's far too late
It's time to clean the slate

Julie Varty, Maryport, Cumbria

BEAUTY IS ONLY SKIN-DEEP

Beauty is only skin-deep
Or so the saying goes
We all have different features
We don't all have the perfect nose

We're all different shapes and sizes
Some are chubby, others very thin
Some have beautiful eyes, others flawless skin
What's really important is the beauty deep within

It's in gifts we have, and may not know it
We may have the gift of music or art
Or the lyrical soul of a poet
What really counts is concealed in our heart

So next time we size someone up in a glance
And their outward appearance is all we are seeing
Just give them a second chance
Look a bit further, to the core of their being

Joan Yates, Preston, Lancashire

MAYBE NOT

We're gonna book a lad's holiday
Going to Benidorm on the lash
Haven't done that in years
It's gonna be a right good bash.

It's gonna be a right laugh
Late nights and good fun
We're gonna hit the discos
Birds, booze and sun.

I'll need some new clothes
Cool shirts and snazzy shorts
I'd better get some condoms
I don't want penile warts.

We're gonna get a tattoo
Same place on the neck
We're the bad lad's army
Benidorm we're gonna wreck.

All night we planned it
We were having loads of drinks
But now it's the morning
I'll have to see what the wife thinks.

Troy Tyne, Clitheroe, Lancashire

BIZARRE CAIRO BAZAAR

They said to us, *It's not recommended*
Stay on the coach, out of harm's way
But my friend and I, we are fearless
And we were only in Cairo one day

So we secured our bags and purses
And set off with a few other *brave souls,*
While our companions watched, air-conditioned
We braved the heat for our goals

It is so cheap, you must have it, a voice said
He said, *Come inside and have tea*
But we've only got thirty minutes
I cried, as he grabbed hold of me

And then without blinking, I'd bought it
And we were soon holding figures galore
So while I wanted a scarab from Cairo
I was leaving with somewhat much more

We never felt endangered or threatened
On our trip to that Cairo bazaar
It's a memory of excitement and laughter
And I just *love* my Sphinx cookie jar

Rachel Butterworth, Burnley, Lancashire

VOYAGE OF DISCOVERY

Well the other day, whilst I was taking a bath,
I looked at my body and I just had to laugh.
There were wrinkles and lines, they were there by the
score,
And my hairline was receding, as never before.

My nails, they were brittle and my hands they were coarse,
In fact, I just felt like an old, knackered cart-horse.
There was no meat on my thighs, and my legs were too thin
And no muscles about, just the skin that held them in.

My jaw-line was sagging, and my eyesight had faded,
It's no wonder, I felt a little bit jaded,
I uttered a moan, and then a loud yell,
My wife came into the bathroom, and said, *I thought you
had fell.*

I said look at this body, and I'll tell you what to do,
When I pass on, just flush what's left down the loo,
Well she stood there beside me, and started to laugh,
And said, the best thing to do, is not to take a bath.

Stan Frankland, Blackpool, Lancashire

INSTILL IN ME

Instill in me
The way life and love
Should be perceived

Take my dreams
And float them downstream
For I no longer believe

Return me back to life
Reciprocate my love
No matter how hard or rife

Proceed forever onwards
March the good march
Wish to hate, none would?

But to carry on regardless
Life's one true mystery
However far the apartness

Instill in me
For the dreams I dream
Instill in me
Everything I could choose to be
Instill in me
What I could achieve

Emma Threlfall, Poulton-le-Fylde, Lancashire

THE DAY I MET GOD

I looked up and saw God looking at me
He was leaning on the roof, very casually
He lifted the hand he was leaning his chin upon
Waved in greeting to me and then he was gone

I looked into a puddle, reflected was God's face
He smiled at me so kindly, with His infinite grace
The wind blew ripples across this watery scene
And then he was gone. I wonder what this can mean?

As I rode from the subway, up the electric-powered stairs
He was there in a poster, he held me in his stare
I went back down the escalator, to once more Him see
But he was gone, replaced by an ad for Typhoo tea

I heard a young man, playing a lamenting saxophone
I had to go and listen as he stood there all alone
He smiled at me as he stopped his melancholy tune
I was frightened he'd mistake me for some sort of crazy
loon

I said, *I'm sorry, but I thought you might be God*
He nodded, not appearing to think this slightly odd
He shook my hand firmly, smiled at me once more
We all are part of Him, of this you can be sure

Dave White, Chorley, Lancashire

A NEW DAY DAWNS

Misty morning
Wet with dew
Shades of pink
And shades of blue

Silent stillness
Fills the air
Senses wake
And now aware

Marshland meadows
Lost in swirls
Mist now moves
The day unfurls

Hills and forests
Come into view
Rising high
In front of you

Early bird song
Seems to say
Silence is broken
Welcome new day

Marian Barker, Preston, Lancashire

MAJESTY

I am not dead,
Now ordained with other roles.
Guardian of life's mossy pathway,
Its pauses and pace.
Silent, silvering circles
Reflect past blossoming
And the fruit I bore.
Divested of my crown of green,
Once the paradise of birds,
Created space for light
Is nature's legacy.
I now greet the burgeoning earth.

Kathy Denton, Horwich, Greater Manchester

DANDELIONS

Gorgon heads above a waving sea of green
Domed, tight-lipped buds, yesterday unseen.

Each turns, blindly, towards the day's eye,
Absorbing vital light and warmth whereby

Petals open, revealing ragged disks of yellow,
Snuggling amidst the velvet, grassy pillow.

A vivid amber glow, a welcome wink,
Encourages anticipating bees to drink

Nectar, pollinate, complete the cycle agreed,
With nature, yielding a spherical pom-pom of seed

Ripe for dispersal. Lawn mowers purr power,
Blades decapitate this wondrous feral flower.

Rona Catterall, Oldham, Greater Manchester

THROUGH THE GLASS DARKLY

Is that my reflection in the mirror?
No, it just can't be.
That dull pale face and sullen look.
No, that isn't me.
My cheeks were golden brown,
My lips so full and red.
So why doth this sad and lonely face,
Stare at me instead?
Oh, but hateful image, I know that you are true,
And why? All because I sold my soul to you.
Those empty, haunted eyes, oh yes they're mine,
Those once filled with love and with happiness did shine.
You scarred my mind, you broke my heart,
You left me dead inside.
With no love, no feeling, no compassion
And no pride.
No reflection in the mirror,
You do not lie.
This world has nothing left for me,
So to it then, goodbye.

Justine A Gibb, Stretford, Greater Manchester

CURTAIN FALL

Curtains drawn, the show is over,
But the crowd doesn't applaud nor disprove.
They just move quietly, slowly out of the room.

They are not discontented, yet there are no enthusiasts.
The loss of affect, feeling, or emotion is disregarding.
A life passed with no significance, not to be remembered.
Just another elapsed soul, wandering through the
darkness.

Cheryl Kelsall, Ashton-under-Lyne, Greater Manchester

MY DAD

I remember my dad, he was rough as they come
As I grew up in Wigan with dad and my mum
He was often unshaven and smelling of booze
And I heard he was slow in paying his dues
Tobacco was never too far from his lips
He liked his fags plain, no fancy cork tips
Those strong manly hands ingrained with coal
Ensured that he never spent time on the dole
He'd go to the club, come home late at night
I could tell from his face he'd been in a fight
We never played cricket or football and such
And dad wasn't much for the tender touch
So I went off to school with my clog irons worn
A hole in my britches and jacket all torn
I'd sit in a corner while dad had his tea
His nose in the paper, he had no time for me
But every so often he'd get up from his chair
Give me a smile and gently ruffle my hair
No words were needed, we knew what we had
My dad was my hero, and I was his lad

R Crispin, Wigan, Greater Manchester

157

POEM FOR A FRIEND

Green is as we were
Before the colours of Cain;
And green is hard to believe in
When poplars outside the window
Stripped of summer's finery
Send wisps of black into the mist.
But wait, only wait and see:
One short month from now, quietly
Soft on the wings of blackbirds
Green will come into its own again;
All around will be green leaves,
Proud, tall grasses bending
Gracefully in a generosity of light.
You and I also will be green again
Sitting in the sun, sipping tea
With children dancing barefoot
Bright and fragrant as flowers.
Only wait and see how gladly
We will forgive this cruel winter
And yearn again for his first snows.

Rakiyah Beswick, Stockport, Greater Manchester

BLACKPOOL

Sea calm, wavelets churning round
a sandbank, oval to lozenge to flat path,
it has disappeared into the sea
and so has the writing in the sand
and sand's proud castles and dams.
In the morning water laps at the wall.

Sun shines brightly, fiercely, all day.
Hotel windows bask. Later, red-faced
sunset across the sea. A giant
takes a coin and scratches the sky,
reveals the full moon, a gold coin.
The prize of the evening.

Rachel Martin, Wigan, Greater Manchester

SMOOTH OPERATOR

His advances were perfect,
His timing precise,
The look in his eyes said it all.

His technique was seductive,
His touch soft and warm,
I knew from the start I would fall.

I tried to resist him
And he knew I would,
What else could I do but accede,

To my lover's caresses,
His ardent embrace?
Just my cat demanding his feed.

Elizabeth Gibson, Stockport, Greater Manchester

IN THOUGHTS OF YOU

Gazing, dreaming, lost,
When my eyes first locked with you.

What are you thinking?
As you stare effortlessly out of the rain-soaked window,
Caressing that perfect cup and saucer as if it was that
Fragile memory you so long to keep hold of.

The room seems so desolate, so lost, like you?

The cover a metaphor?
Waiting for the touch of a new owner to uncover its
precious jewels,
Like you, perhaps?

I long to sit where you are and look out,
See what you feel and watch what you see.
Is it Jack, perhaps?

Smile, yes. You take pride of place in my home,
Every day I fall into your dream and catch a glimpse of
what could be.

Nicola Wilcock, Irlam, Greater Manchester

FINAL DESTINATION

Thames water reflects ancient and new,
locks and ships, and a bottleneck whale.

He did not expect hospitality,
photo shoots and eagerness,
to take him back to sea.

They moved him downstream,
constantly bathing him,
'til the unbearable truth,
his days had come to an end.

This was no basking whale,
it was looking for a resting place,
but that was not to be,
for man had to intervene,
ship him back, he is a foreigner.

Like an asylum seeker,
what instincts brought
him to ground, may have been
the desire to quietly
die away from the seas.

Robert Namushi, Rochdale, Greater Manchester

MOTHMAN

Alone I sit, transfixed by the glow of my drink,
Absorbing the sounds;
Clinking glasses and unrequited passes.

I'm joined by a thought,
A peculiar sort,
Taking a sip then releasing a cough,
Realising I'd changed form,
Into that of a moth.

For you see not in body or any aesthetic,
It's much more demeaning,
Undeniably pathetic.

I've acquired the mind of the moth,
A mind refusing to learn,
While her light is attractive, it will eventually burn.

Luring me in with a vivid array of colour and beauty,
She's a double-edged sword of both excitement and cruelty.

I've been scorched too often by this womanly flame,
Getting close is too deadly a game.

Joseph Bailey, Heywood, Greater Manchester

GARBAGE

There were crisp packets,
Broken glass, condoms too,
Not to mention the needles and dog poo.
Boarded up windows,
Mangled tyres,
Dirty old mattresses
And twisted barbed wire.
Screaming graffiti with anger and pain.
Greyness, poverty, depression and rain.
Yet, amongst the garbage, something grew,
A bursting bud, fresh and new.
To think that I did almost pass
This gift of hope in the tufts of grass.

Wendy Black, Liverpool, Merseyside

GOLDEN ANGEL

Bright golden hair,
Hazy brown eyes,
Body so fine,
Spirit shining bright.
Under the lights he sings,
Serenades my heart,
Unknown to him
My love blossoms,
Calling,
Falling at his feet.
My golden angel,
My shining star,
Will you ever see,
Just how bright my love
Does shine?

Susan Pope, Liverpool, Merseyside

THE TEENAGER

Could anybody love him but his mother?
Morose, round-shouldered, lazy, selfish brute.
Could anybody care a toss about him?
He's good for nothing, that's the awful truth.

Have sixteen years of training taught him nothing?
Uncouth, ill-mannered, inconsiderate lout.
Would anybody want to share his company?
They'd lock him up and never let him out.

His room exceeds your worst imagination,
With dirty clothes and socks thrown on the floor.
There's coffee cups and greasy plates and dishes
And magazines, crisp packets there galore.

And who on earth can be this monster's mother?
Could she be really fond of such a son?
And does she now regret she ever had him,
Despise him for the awful things he's done?

I must confess that I'm this monster's mother.
You ask if I could love him, yes, I could.
And do I now regret I ever had him?
The answer's plain, it's no, I never would.

Dorothy Parry, Southport, Merseyside

THE LAND OF LITTLE PEOPLE

There is a land where children go,
Beyond the church and steeple,
To the edge of the world and back again,
To the land of little people,
Where roads are covered in chocolate cream,
Rivers flow with pop,
And forests abound with lollipop trees
With lots of cream on top.
There are woods and lakes and magic spells
And fairies in the park,
And elves and gnomes of every kind,
To chase away the dark.
It's a world of tears and laughter,
Which every child knows well,
The golden land of make believe
With its ageless magic spell.
But no one knows its whereabouts,
The direction that it lies,
Though the gateway's there for all to see
In children's shining eyes.

Ed Collins, Southport, Merseyside

North
East

LOOKING BACK

What did you do in the war, nanna?
Youngest grandchild said to me.
Well, not very much really,
I was only seven you see.
But I told her about the sirens
And the gas-masks that we wore,
And how we had to grow our own food,
For we could not import anymore.
My grandparents had a small-holding
And had a large garden as well,
So I helped feed the pigs and the chickens
And collect the eggs to sell.
I weeded in the garden
And staked up beans and peas,
And picked up fallen apples
From underneath the trees.
So when I think about it,
Whether big or small,
It's good I did the little jobs.
I did my bit after all.

Janette Coverdale, Middlesbrough, Cleveland

6.30 A.M.

Freshly baked bread moves through the air above
Pavement slabs, for the shortest time warming it,
But only just.

The air is cold, but still there is the smallest amount
Of condensation on the outside of the plastic bottle,
Because the milk is colder, but only just.

The folded newspaper holds its tongue for the moment,
Waiting for the chance to impress with its hot news,
Ink now dry, but only just.

Worn shoes, to which feet have adjusted over
Many months, make it to the bedsit without stepping on
The cracks, but only just.

Silence and loneliness jostle while the paper is read,
Waiting to reclaim control of their victim. It's a life,
But only just.

Neil Posselwhite, Loftus, Cleveland

GOING GREEN

I'm going to save the planet. I'm going to go bright green.
My garden will be the eco-est the world has ever seen.

I rang the local council,
They sent a compost bin
So now I've got to sort the things
That I can put within.

I know I can use carrots,
Potato and apple peel,
But what about the cold remains
Of last night's Chinese meal?

Egg boxes and grass clippings
Should quickly biodegrade,
So I will hurl them in
From my brand new, shiny spade.

But will a host of buzzy flies
Hover around the bin?
Will it attract a swarm of ants?
And will the rats move in?

It all seems complicated, and the sky looks very grey
And I'm feeling rather weary, so I'll start ... another day.

Kathleen Brown, Darlington, County Durham

LIFE'S SEASONS

The spring of life,
Young limbs that play
The childish games
And laughter fills the day.

Then summer is here
And love and zest hold sway,
To plan and endeavour,
To succeed, come what may.

Autumn brings the quiet time,
To comprehend your graces,
To look at life in tranquil mood,
In whatever state it places.

Winter starts with a glow,
Then dims as living slows.
Long shadows seem to dim the eyes,
Yet see much as they close.

Bill Burnett, Stockton-on-Tees, County Durham

LIVING LOVE

You are my wholeness,
Without you I am lacking
Those finer details, the smoother edges,
The smallest, vital cog in my most complex workings.
You are the punctuation in the book of my life,
Bringing meaning and value to the randomness of words.
You bring to life my screenplay,
Directing it with compassion and love,
To show the purpose in my reality.
My ordered world is disordered by the intrusion of your will
And I am not afraid.

I relish your presence in my life and treasure beyond all
things,
This coming close to you.
Without you I have only things
Which neither last nor satisfy beyond an earthly scale,
But with you, I have the very earth itself;
The sun and the moon and all the stars,
The universe and the heavens are mine to hold.
Not in the hand of my humaness,
But in the heart of my completeness.

Ann Wilson, Chester-le-Street, County Durham

SOLUNAR

A drawn out battle,
throughout the land.
Between two bodies,
going hand in hand.
The aim for each,
the other to die.
To reign supreme,
king of the sky.

One brings light,
the other shade.
Courses plotted,
foundations laid.
Continuous cycle,
arriving soon.
A war between,
the sun and the moon.

David Tobin, Chilton, County Durham

THE DEPARTURE

I never knew him
But I'm haunted by him
I picture him
Holding his mother
Telepathically saying he loves her
Saying his final goodbye
He knows that it's over
That he's leaving forever
She doesn't know
She's just holding the son
That she bore, that she loves
Puzzled by his unexpected affection
But not questioning it too deeply
As she hopes that tomorrow
She'll be holding him again
But she won't
Because he'll have gone
Gone for good

Lorraine Facey, Crook, County Durham

A BLANK PAGE

A blank page filled with words,
Is a victory,
A pen without ink,
Is a shame,
An end to a ream of thoughts,
Would make a story,
A loss is a thoughtful image,
Without a name,
The easiest form of magic,
Is a poem,
A scribble on a scrapbook,
Is a start,
For in these dreamy dwellings,
Is a home,
To rest the weary wand'rings,
Of the heart.

Stephanie Gillespie, Durham, County Durham

ROUND

The sea breaks everything in time
And when everything is broken,
It reforms mud, bone and slime.
The smallest grains of shell and sand
Are compressed to layers of stone,
The world is rebuilt, and the tide rolls on.

The earth spews fire from her heart,
Rocks melt, and continents drift apart.
But the sea cools and the oceans mend,
Dust settles and the sky clears in the end.
The air freshens and the clouds grow,
Rain falls and the rivers flow.

The world sprouts her mantle green,
Trees flourish, flowers bloom, animals abound,
Reproduction makes the world go round.
But, the sea breaks everything in time,
Stones, bones, metal and wood
And the hearts of men who misunderstood.

Arneil Rutherford, High Shincliffe, County Durham

SOLITARY SOLUTION

My solitude,
I live in emptiness,
The searchlights looking for me
To cast a shadow across my face.

My silhouette,
Against the moon,
A magnet for the insane,
Attracting the unattractive.

My description,
The picture's never quite finished,
There's always a piece missing,
Like memories in the mist.

My ego,
Is on fire
And the ashes fall from my face,
Revealing the truth.

My reflection,
Pulling out my hair
And turning the other cheek
But never backing down.

Michael Brett, Newbiggin-by-the-Sea, Northumberland

TRANSITIONS

Many memories are stuffed inside of
The dusty drawer of my unconscious mind,
Because with swift and savage succession
Years were soon lost in the midst of time.

Long ago I had the speed of a juggler,
The dexterity of a magician each day,
But the incredible complexities of morality,
Stole the exuberance of my youth away.

My once frenetic chaos and confusion,
Replaced by enlightenment of simplicity,
Peace and well-being that nourishes the soul,
Psychiatric healing of middle-aged mediocrity.

We are all at the mercy of circumstances
And the paramount concerns of youth decline,
Yet a sense of liberation overwhelms me,
My transition earnestly embraced through time.

Snatched cellular moments of my photographs
Retain evidence of how things used to be,
Constant reminders that nothing lasts forever,
Yet inside I am still the whimsical, ebullient me.

Celia Auld, Ashington, Northumberland

PATHWAYS OF LIFE

Walk slowly along life's pathways,
Take in each sight and every sound,
Cherish each moment you're given,
As life only comes once around.
Relish the wonders of sunset,
Watch a brand new day begin,
The smell of earth's fragrant flowers,
The feel of the sun on your skin.
The smile you get from a baby,
Plus the love that children all bring,
Icicles that sparkle in winter,
The blossom of bough in the spring.
As you grow from a child to an adult,
From a girl to a woman and wife,
Treasure each moment you're given,
As you walk through
The pathways of life.

Brenda Thurlbeck, Sunderland, Tyne and Wear

ELEGY IN A POOR CHURCHYARD

For these no more the early Naughties clarions
Depressing news of social intercourse
As revelations of each starlet's carry-ons
Inure to lying, cheating and divorce.

Their day's first fix at half-awakened morn,
Brown ale, buckfast, or other special brews.
Or distillation of fermented corn,
No more need brace them for jobseekers' queues.

But gentle reader, tempted to condemn,
Consider these Rab Nesbitts were but learners,
Remember daily hearing on P.M.
Of *fat cats*, making much on *little earners*?

For while the titled rich in boardrooms plush,
Consort with MPs while they wheel and deal,
These simple poor, in pastures much less lush,
Just ducked and dived with others down at heel.

It may be here lie some who could not cope,
Whoe'er their kinsfolk ordered up morticians,
Have used their crafty talents, given scope
And helped themselves as, *honest politicians.*

Patrick Brady, Whitley Bay, Tyne and Wear

HUMAN GEOLOGY

There are people I do not know
but parts of them
are with me.
They are my blood,
my hair colour,
my eyes,
which are windows
to my soul.
Through the years
I am an image
of all of them.
Piece by piece,
vein by vein,
cell by cell,
I am me,
because of them.
Layer upon layer,
A human strata.

Eileen Burns, Newcastle-upon-Tyne, Tyne and Wear

MIDNIGHT

The clock begins to strike, each tone reverberating through
an ink-black sky.
A sky where the suspended disc of dappled moon hovers,
encircled by hazy diffusions of light.
A sky littered with stars, sparkling like strings of fairy
lights scattered across the heavens.
Far below, late summer flowers shiver under frosted leaves,
Frosted leaves fallen from trees that now stand bare and
gaunt.
Their gnarled branches reach skywards, casting eerie
shadows across silvered grass.
Jewels of breath escape from an unknown figure and hang
wisp-like in the air before they disappear.
No wind disturbs the cold stillness of the night,
No birdsong cheers the chilled air.
Midnight chimes,
All is still.
The day has ended,
Dawn is far away.

Sandi Readhead, Hull, East Yorkshire

IONA

An island there is in the distant north,
Set as a diamond in the turquoise seas
And to that place we pilgrims did set forth

On our long journey. Facing the strong breeze
Our fragile barque ploughed bravely through the night,
For safe deliverance, prayed we on our knees.

At last we reached the land, O wondrous sight!
Ten thousand saints were waiting on the shore.
Around them shone a pure, celestial light.

Those holy souls that have gone on before
Were there to welcome us among the stones
And we, with them, shall stay forevermore.

The saints and kings who left behind their bones,
Are raised to glory now, upon their thrones.

Christine McLaren, Keyingham, East Yorkshire

LONG DAYS

Long, long the days
I spent alone
Within the pain
Of these four walls.
Who can escape the sorrow
Found within?
The pain of looking out
With sightless eyes,
Despairing
Of the smells of spring,
Sweet blossoms,
Love and everything.
To savour pain without regret
Was much too hard for me
And yet I cannot think
Of days gone by,
Without an ache of pain
And some regret.

Richard Pooley, Hull, East Yorkshire

THE CAVE

From daylight to darkness
It came to me quite a shock
As I entered a maze of caves
Which were made of solid rock

The walls were practically side by side
Leaving a very small gap
Placing my hands in front of me
Someone must have turned on a tap

Water cascaded down, cold and wet
My clothes did not stand a chance
Everything felt so slimy
It was as though I was in a trance

A glimmer of light could be seen ahead
My heart leapt with joy at the sight
Never again would this venture occur
When I reached the end, I took a flight

Sylvia Varley, York, North Yorkshire

I WISH

I wish I could walk the hills again
Under the blue arch of sky.
Or stand there on a windy day,
See cloud shadows scudding by.

I wish I could walk the woods again,
See the magic springtime weaves.
Or see the glory of autumn's colours,
Walk the carpet of fallen leaves.

I wish I could walk the valleys again,
See broad fields dotted white
With newborn lambs, bleating,
Running, springing from sheer delight.

I wish I could walk the fields again,
Follow the footpaths wherever they go
And see shy violets on grassy banks
And primroses' delicate, yellow glow.

I wish I could walk in pleasant towns
And visit places I used to find,
But those days are gone forever
And they're only pictures in my mind.

Margaret Kirkup, Pickering, North Yorkshire

TRANCE

Lying awake at night,
Tormented by nightmare dreams,
Haunted by shadows,
The world's not as it seems.

Running from demons,
Inner peace far from sight,
Fierce storms drawing close,
Trying hard to find the light.

Searching for hidden paths,
In a forest of broken dreams,
Leading out to a sunrise,
The chance to be redeemed.

Vicky Garlick, Ripon, North Yorkshire

THE GARDENER

A gardener was heard to mutter,
My garden shed is full of clutter.
He often vowed to throw away,
Then save it for a rainy day.
Items that were all the rage,
Now victims of a bygone age;
Ancient mowers leaking oil,
Well-used tools to till the soil.
Decaying bulbs and seeds galore,
Plant pots strewn across the floor.
Tins of paint of every hue,
Ditched that shade in eighty-two.
Dirty macs and paperbacks,
Newspapers and hessian sacks.
How does he find what's in his shed?
The answer lies within his head.

Robert Hill, Ripon, North Yorkshire

YOU IN ME

I saw your face in mine
Today, in the mirror,
There it was.
The eyes, now slightly hooded,
The chin achieving prominence,
Two folds from nose to mouth,
Incipient, it's true,
But there.
Your face in mine.

Not a young woman
Any more,
Still less the girl
I was,
The day you died.

Today, in the mirror,
Your maleness in me,
Living on,
Not gone.
I see your face in mine.

Audrey McIlvain Jefferson, Scarborough, North Yorkshire

DANCE UPON MY GRAVE

If I return from this valley of hell with sealed eyes
and silent heart, do not weep that I am sleeping,
be merry, for I sleep beneath English skies.
If I am fallen when sweet victory raiseth her head,
do not shed one sorrowful tear nor mourn my absence,
for I lie with the glorious dead.
On armistice day, lay no flowers for the buried brave,
for how shall we know that peace is come?
Wake me sweet with long waited news
and dance upon my grave.

Andrea Mitchell, Thirsk, North Yorkshire

MISTRESS ULLSWATER

Looking across Ullswater to the fells beyond
Hung like a backcloth engraved in time
Lines etched on its face like an old woman's, yet
With breathtaking beauty unrefined

Great expanse of water, steely blue and deep
With gulls wheeling and skimming
Leaving their harsh cries hanging on the wind
Torn, jagged and wild
Whole colonies out there, away from the shore
Filling me with such wondrous awe

Mallard duck and coot, riding the white caps
Whipped up into peaks
Countless magnetic fathoms mocking
Throwing her head in haughty contempt
Flashing her eyes at the lonely traveller
I turned away, feeling uneasy, unable to rest
Mistress Ullswater is today at her best

Barbara Price, Escrick, North Yorkshire

TEARS OF ASH

She lives so lifeless now, laying in the dark
So very painful, nursing a burnt-out trembling heart
The mouths that spoke they damned her, the fingers that
touched her tainted
The minds that raised her thoughtless, though she never
cursed or hated.

She lays so fallen, bled and still
Oh, of this life she's had her fill
She exists so fragile, so drained and so pale
For she is the sufferer, of such a tragic tale.

For they stoked their hatred, in form of fire
Burnt down honest hope, torched down every spire
Now she has fallen, she lies crumbling in the dirt
She deserved no such suffering, she deserves no such hurt.

For her suffering she's confused, understand she never
could
The end it is looming, her wrists weep in blood
Her inner self, it burns, burns an ugly gash
Her final sigh ironic, she's crying tears of ash.

Mark Turvey, Doncaster, South Yorkshire

PEACE IN THE STORM

Wind howling o'er the moor
Rain lashing against the door
Window pane madly rattling
The storm furiously battling.
Clock ticking on the mantel
The guttering of a candle
Rocking chair gently creaking
The fire quietly flickering.
Clicking needles steadily knitting
And old woman peacefully sitting.

Carol Phillips, North Anston, South Yorkshire

HULL POT

Unguarded entrance to an arcane underworld
of gill and fall, cavern and corridor
this limestone pot-hole gashes the grassy floor
of undulating foothills, dimly furled
with ribs of rock ascending to the heights
where grey sheep graze in isolated stealth.

A carefree browser, relishing the wealth
of pasture there, edged forward with her sights
on one blade more - too far! She slithered down
the slope, the scree, the sheer drop of the cliff
of that vast hull-shaped hollow of renown
and perished, her bare bones gleaming in the rift.

O man! Beware the slide that leads to hell
and heed your conscience as a warning bell.

David Jardine, Sheffield, South Yorkshire

LOOK BEYOND

Look beyond the silver hair, look into my eyes
And see the young man behind the blank stare.
The man who had feelings, the man who cared,
The man who played football, the man who shared.

The man who enjoyed a pint, on a Saturday night,
The man who helped put all the wrong things right,
The man who fixed things, when they went wrong,
The man who whistled a tuneless song.

The man who worked hard each day of the week
Without a grumble, so we could seek
Our destiny.

As we grew into adulthood, the man who was once
Your father, your brother,
The man who meant everything to you like no other.
I am still there,
Look deep into my eyes, I am still there,
The young man behind
The silver hair.

Mary Drost, Halifax, West Yorkshire

NOCTURNAL VISION

In a darkened wood, wide eyes peeped,
Through rustling leaves, hidden from view.
Just waiting, waiting,
He sees all.

Life passes by, not knowing.
Momentary without a care, unaware.
Biding time, biding time,
So still is he.

Night-time manoeuvres soon to commence,
A sudden surge of movement, effortlessly,
Swooping, swooping,
Swift, so swift.

Vision of strength, beauty and wisdom,
With a strange turn of the head.
Gliding, gliding,
Hunter bold.

The shining moon seeps through and winks,
In charge of the woods, the wise one returns,
To survey, survey
And he hoots, hoots.

Pauline Hardman, Leeds, West Yorkshire

JUST ME

Consequently,
As you see,
Nothing much became of me.
I never wrote
That classic book,
Never had what it took.
Never really
Took a stand,
Not done very much that's grand.
Didn't discover
Anything new,
Times I impressed? Very few.
Cannot say
I'm celebrity,
Far too busy with drudgery.
In fact
I've lived an ordinary life,
Just mother, sister, daughter, wife.

Cecilia Brabin, Pudsey, West Yorkshire

TREMOR

There came a great stillness.
The earth held its breath.
No birdsong, no rustle of leaf,
No ripple disturbed the glass lake.

All life at a standstill
And I couldn't move.
Ears and eyes strained for the coming,
Each creature aware and awake.

There was fear in the air,
My senses alert.
As shivers ran over the mere
And I felt the first trembling shake.

Alarm in the grasses,
The blank and the trees,
The birds startled calls as they rose
From the unseen cause of the quake.

Expectant and fearful,
I waited for more,
But nature returned to its calm,
Dismissing earth's minor mistake.

Patricia Farley, Keighley, West Yorkshire

STARLINGS

They have been gathering
all afternoon

A skin
of sentinels
on every roof-top

A racketing shriek
comes in at the windows

At five-seventeen
with an inaudible drum-roll
they are in the sky

Spiralling
obsessed with order
a cloud-lung
of wings

Gasping in crescendo
over winter sand

Children run down the prom
breathless
and free

Suzannah Evans, Leeds, West Yorkshire

WEATHERING THE STORM

A new day dawns with a glimmer of sunlight,
I open my eyes and dare to hope,
Is this the day that the storm will break?
I sense the tension and feel the electricity rising,
Scurrying dark clouds obliterate the light.

The hope has gone and it's raining again.

A piercing shower, like needles, makes me shiver,
Temperatures fall as I anticipate the final strike.
The world illuminates in a brilliant flash of light,
Stealing my breath away.

The storm has returned and seeks me out,
Overpowering me with its persistence and strength.
Somebody is reaching out to me with a comforting hand
And the shelter is now within my grasp.

I struggle to accept the help, fighting the eye of the storm.
Gradually the medication works and
I have weathered the storm of pain again,
For a while.

Elaine Bamford, Otley, West Yorkshire

196

LAST DAYS OF AUTUMN

I see autumn in its waning days,
Now trees, unclothed, look quite forlorn.
Fallen leaves withered and early dawn
So bare of face, no chorus now
Of pert blackbird or warbling thrush,
Only the hush of deep, deep silence
And echoes of dreams forever lost.
Corn stubble fields and November mists,
Unheathered moors and hedgerows bare,
The dying year is everywhere.

Is this the place that stirred my heart,
That is now stark, a cold closed door?
Now I could weep for all that beauty,
The youthful days that are no more
And would it not have been more kind
To dull my memories of this barren time?
Then I may live without sad dreaming,
No more that deep ache in my heart,
No more to mourn this desolation,
See out the old without lamentation.

Barbara Robinson, Boston Spa, West Yorkshire

Wales

THE GRAVEL PIT

The gravel pit, mirror smooth and morning still,
Reflecting red schoolhouse roof and willows green.
Footprints on frosty grass, fences cobweb frill,
Crunchy cornflake leaves, and conker's glossy sheen.

The gravel pit, bird ruffled as now bestirred
By coots playing noughts and crosses, or landing
With water-skiing feet. The grebe, unperturbed,
Dive deftly and return, punk hair upstanding.

The gravel pit, tufty sprinkled thickly far,
And near, goose flotillas calm at anchor lie.
Not so the swans, hissing and stretching to bar
The stranger. Mallard swim with their mates close by

The gravel pit, red tinted with sunset glow
Lies beneath the roost returning flocks that call.
Two cormorants fly quickly, the heron slow,
Flaps into the dusk-grey, misty even-fall.

Jo Brookes, Newcastle Emlyn, Wales

MY HERO

He was as gentle as the grass he trod
Soft and warm as a summer morning breeze
He came to me, sent maybe by God
When, like a lost sailor I sailed the seas
While the drifting boat faced each high wave
The storm slashed its fury to tear it apart
No harbour light shown, no light it ever gave
Heavy was the burden, broken the heart
When all hope was lost, just like in my dream
The storm subsided, the harbour light shown
Strong, bright, comforting its rescuing beam
He came so life began, the battle won
For twenty three years I worshipped him
The hero as gentle as the grass he trod

Carolina Rosati-Jones, Swansea, Wales

SNOWSTORM OVER KILIMANJARO

How can the days we shared
Ever escape from my memory?
As beautiful as a snowstorm
Over the mighty Kilimanjaro
Replenishing the thawing glacier
If only for a fleeting while.

How can your memory ever fade?
I'll forever recall faraway eyes and lips
More fragrant than the sweetest ambrosia
But then at least I've explored
A magical land some never manage to view
As beautiful as a snowstorm
Over the mighty Kilimanjaro range
Yet now only exquisite memories remain.

Guy Fletcher, Cardiff, Wales

SUMMER'S STAGE

Oh, sweet daffodils I watch
You grow
And bend below the weight
Of snow
This winter cloak of white
Upon you
Until the sun its warmth
Caresses
Now your golden trumpet is
Held high
To face a bright and clear
Sky
Until once more your head is
Bowed with age
Yet. That sets the summer
Stage
Of flowers wild in blooms
Of colour
That heralds in a brand new
Summer

Ken Millard, Newport, Wales

THE WORD CONDUCTOR

She breezes in ready for action
Marker in hand, ready to control the orchestra
We are going on a journey today
She says
So fasten your seatbelts, let's not delay, and enjoy the ride
She says
If you're not committed, you'd better hide
But we are on her side
You know
She is the word conductor who makes our language
Electrons flow
So our love of words will pour out onto our own
Orchestras one day

Jon Roberts, Holywell, Wales

A CHILD'S BEDROOM

Like some small temple, this bedroom shines
The freshly painted pastel walls reflect the occupant
So clean and new
One day, the same walls will throb to the latest beat
Be background to badly taken photographs
Treasured tickets of a much-loved show
Home to worn out teddy bears
Or house a bruised and aching heart
It is then you will tiptoe in (knock first)
Step carefully around the unwashed clothes
Half empty mugs to give advice, but don't
For now let time stand still
The hour is a pearl
The room is a jewel
This bedroom shines

Sarah Williams, Denbigh, Wales

WEEPERS IN GRIEF

The estuary can be seen from this window, even at night
time
The horizon's moods change with daylight slipping away
Yet tomorrow will delight and thrill my soul as once again
I gaze with awe at this marvellous sight

Turmoil, the undercurrent of grief
Will I ever be free of it?
How we sour love with petty jealousy and addiction to
needless dramas
Such folly, desperately seeking love by any name

When will we learn to trust life a bit more?
Is the wisdom of the ancients dead in our hearts?
Drunk on greed, pawing for self-survival and power-mad
leaders
Full of broken promises given to the children
Who sold their souls for the medals of the dead sons of
weeping women

The estuary can be seen from this window, even at night
time
I gaze with awe at this marvellous sight
And I remember you

Pat Dryden, Holywell, Wales

MIDNIGHT TOIL

I pull the bedclothes o'er my head
To blanket out the bleats
Of passing sunrise citizens
Whose speech my slumbers breach
Despite their apprehensions
I saw the sunrise too
The midnight oil burned low and red
How silently the night had sped
Like morning dew my writings spread
Before my weary eyes of lead
To bed I tread, lay down my head
My spirit to renew

Lynda Howell, Haverfordwest, Wales

TO IVY, THE GARDENS OF REMEMBRANCE AT EASTER

Ivy, the flowers that you sell
Have, for your buyers, much to tell
Not only a wondrous, glorious array
They have much more to us to say
Beauty is their greatest asset
But each petal is a special facet
Showing sadness of loss, but giving hope
So rich in love, helping us cope
Carrying memories, promise giving
Wrongs wiped away, in forgiving
As Easter's cross reveals God's love
So flowers, His gift too from above
Inspire and cheer, lift one's heart
Bearing a smile, to play their part
Ivy, that is what you're selling
That is what each bloom is telling

Arthur Hughes, Llandudno, Wales

UNRAVELLED

The sky at night unravels
Silver threads hang from her hem
Shooting stars they travel
Through deep blue velvet
Nature's gems
The crescent moon like a smile
Beaming wide, into the night
When unveiled its glory shines
And woodlands bathe
In silver light

Ian William Morley, Monmouth, Wales

YOU AND I

One lingering kiss is all I need
To tell me you are mine
Replacing all the pecks you gave
When first we were entwined

Your timid touch, your faltering lips
No longer let you down
And now you have the confidence
To laugh and tease and frown

And now we are together
As happy as the larks
We're soaring and we're singing
Oblivious of the past

We're arm in arm and hand in hand
As all things pass us by
We're drunk as lords with happiness
And life's an endless high

Anne Marie Lawrence, Treorchy, Wales

ETERNITY

A stranger came to my abode
And rapped upon my door
He said his name was Victory
And he'd come here no more

But I was younger then
And drank his chalice dry
Then onward to Eternity
Went Victory and I

The journey long and arduous
Asphalt, turned to ragged stone
Sweet Victory abandoned me
And left me there alone

A stranger came to my abode
And rapped upon my door
He said his name was Jesus Christ
And he'd come here no more

But I was so much older then
And drank his chalice dry
So onward to Eternity
Went Jesus Christ and I

Roger M Robson, Swansea, Wales

SHRIMPS

All of my life I've been followed by shrimps
They stand at street corners like out of work pimps
They celebrate their lives beneath brown trilby hats
They stalk me in moonlight by avoiding the cats

All of my life I've been followed by shrimps
They wear Harry Brown's they pretend to have limps
They breakfast in cafe's while grooming their lashes
They're peanuts on sticks wearing joke shop moustaches

Riaz Ali, Cwmbran, Wales

ADVERSITY'S ADVANTAGE

Adversity is advantage
There's power in your pain
When your broken heart is mended
You'll never grieve again

The mystery in your misery
Is that when it is reversed
The wounds of your suffering
Will never again be nursed

You'll reach out with your heart towards others
Who are facing the same sorrow and grief
You'll put loving arms around them
And bring them some relief

With compassion you will walk with strength
Down the old road of the past again
But the only thing you'll cry about
Will be other people's pain

Sara Reardon, Newport, Wales

207

Northern Ireland

CRIME AND PUNISHMENT

Witness, evidence, scene of crime
Copper, lawyer, I'm given time
Handcuffs, prison van, twenty foot wall
Gates close, locks slam, reception hall
Officers surround me, uniform blue
Ten foot cell, little to do
Recreation, foodhall, lockup, lights out
Drug abuse, phone cards, messing about
Prison chaplain, education, sentence review
Parole board, criminal justice, appeals few
Punishment delivered, freedom curtailed
Life is on hold, train is derailed
Offender, criminal, no hope, waste of space
Judge sent me down, fifteen years in this place

Jennifer Carlisle, Comber, Northern Ireland

WILD WOOD HYACINTH

Tall, green canopies rise like parasols from the aeons of leaf
mould that cover the ground
Their leaves, a myriad of hues
The lungs of the world
Their cover, gently protecting a new growth of green,
shooting up through the damp, brown epidermis of the
earth
It's bluebell time
Those seemingly delicate, soft, blue trumpets belie a
steeliness within them
Their distinctive perfume carried on a soft breeze through
the native woodland of oak and beech
Of sycamore and ash and horse chestnut
The striking medley of blue and green, an oasis of calm and
beauty
Their inherent resurgence, a joy always to my heart

Heather McCracken, Newtownards, Northern Ireland

WILD WHITE ROSE

To touch the treasure of your soul
Give pleasure to your eyes
To lie within your loving hands
Is what I most desire

Let others see my colder side
The stab they would feel
Blood would be a full reward
If from your hand they try to steal

In truth I am a flower that shines
For you to have and hold
My heart I give so freely
To you my softest thorns

Hard against the storms of life
Much like the moon's full glow
In gentle petals of full blossom
I am a wild white rose

Albert Whiteside, Belfast, Northern Ireland

DISAPPEAR

Was it a dress of flies
She expected like a plant
To fuse herself into.
To decompose like snow,
Waiting in the sun
For resolution,
Sleep herself to freedom
Underground in silence
Like a window shut,
Never out of scene.

Wilting in summer
Famous in her winter
Her suicide in the paper.

Ande Milligan, Omagh, Northern Ireland

I HAVE KNOWN LOVE

I have known love and been loved
Took its hand and strolled thro' summers
Passions and jealousies
Held it in my hand
As I cried out
Wept when it wept
O
I have known love
Now autumn has fallen
I walk on dead leaves
My love's no longer
Who will take my red rose
Now summer's no longer
And autumn leaves fall
O
I have known love

William Crawford, Ballywalter, Northern Ireland

THE WREN

The dry dead stalks o'erspread the sloping bank.
Withered and lifeless they lay askew.
Last summer tall and green with pink florets,
Now prone and brittle waiting growth anew.

As I stood gazing there and pondered life,
A gentle rustling, intermittent, drew
Me nearer, stopping low beside the stream.
Silence reigned and expectation grew.

I held my breath; I scarcely dared to move,
Peering intently tangled tendrils through.
Then just beyond, close to the water's edge
A tiny upright tail flicked into view.

It was a dainty wren, whose lonely ways
The leaning balsam canes' protecting hue
Covered. Lost in drab brown stems it searched
With flitting movements, insects black and blue.

Below, its pale reflection - upside down,
On sluggish water showed. Then off it flew.
Oh busy wren! Our pathways briefly crossed,
You intent on lunch, and I on you.

Joan-Pamela Moore, Londonderry, Northern Ireland

AFTER THE VISIT

The house was bright tonight,
It seemed to swell and fill with pride;
Its face took on a fresher look as though
It took itself in hand to seem more welcoming
And grand because you came tonight

There was a warmth, a newness, a well-nourished air
That flowed from walls and windows, and the stairs
Seemed wider than before and far less steep
And the old carpet's pile seemed soft and deep

Your presence gave the house a special splendour,
The things that were so ordinary before -
The shabby rug, chipped paint, the old armchair -
Were brought at once alive when you were there

The hours went past so swiftly when you came
I would have shut the door on time
To make your visit last the longer, if I could,
But all that's good must end and time march on.

I watched you walk away,
The ending of another day, another visit over;
I waved you off and turned into the house again -
The dead, dull house that shrank in upon itself
Back into the shell of ordinariness, the glow all gone.

Betty McIlroy, Bangor, Northern Ireland

WHAT CAN I SAY?

I cannot beg to be heard or be heard without begging
For an ebb in the flow of rage
A lifetime of mothering, a withering harvest unblessed

What ruins do you seek of houses never built
And things of beauty made monstrous in your dreaming?
My voice is silent, yet I grow devil horns
Your voice is raging, yet you grow angel wings

I have been here before a weary physician
Hands fumbling in the dark to channel healing
To light the night between us

All birds think they are free in cages, built in the name of
love
A life measured by a wingspan, determined by their
captor's fears

If I were to state his limitations it would weigh against me
For the judge and juror weigh their own soul
Let the seasons deliver their autumn and spring will follow
Between us
I pray for a space
Where love can unfold its wings

Pia Gore, Bangor, Northern Ireland

Scotland

LIFE

Life is at my feet
And I keep standing on it
Its face so often flattened
And yet it still smiles
Even when my tears
Wash off the make-up
Leaving lines of time
And memory
Cover them up quickly
I'm only young
Reality is tough
And even worse stripped
Naked of its cushions
Kiss me quickly
Hold me tightly
In thy cobweb
Breathe down this emptiness
Till death dissolves
The glue
And claims me His

Colette Chadha, Gordon, Scotland

NEVER HAD

Never had no gunfire roaring at my door
Never had no dead child lying on the floor
Never had to walk away from the place that I call home
Never had to leave my land and evermore to roam

Never had no luck, you say
No fortune smiles on us
Just tell that to these other folks
Whose lives have turned to dust

I Elder, Kelso, Scotland

CLOUDS

Resting recumbent on my back,
way off the track
I focused upwards on the jostling clouds,
imagining crowds
of hippopotami, or floating herds
of elephants or polar bears or giant birds
shape-shifting so fast
no single one of them destined to last.

Dependent on planetary spin, of course,
and held by that force
allegedly the source of Newton's laws
I had to pause
to wonder if I might be upside down,
the clouds beneath.

Imagine, if that grip were once withdrawn
I'd end up plunging to my death,
emptied of breath,
under those trampling, vaporous feet.

Ken Angus, Gorebridge, Scotland

DOWN AND OUT IN THE CASTLEGATE

Sky swept sadness haunts the mind
And shoulders heavy with neglect
Huddle in the Castlegate in cold drizzled
Mists of grey granite.
Word tired mouths spit blasphemes
Across wooden benches
Their twisted bodies, folding
Like withered parchments
Drink the air around them
Their wine-drenched lips
Kiss at nippled glass
Drip tears of meth-blown madness
And feed at the city's alcoholic breast
With vacant eyes they stumble
Their reflections trapped in wet cobblestones
Fail to hear the echoes of worlds
That once belonged to them
She watches them, knows their wanting
Offers cold sanctuary among her pigeons
She the Castlegate, nurses her children

Josephine Duthie, Aberdeen, Scotland

TRUSTING A SPARROW

If you only knew what I had done to gain your trust
To fly upon the wings of a sparrow
Up here so high
Would you send me back to earth if I failed to gain your
heart?
Would let me depart with cold winds at my back?
Or would you let the setting sun rise another day
And let me fly so high so high
Upon the wings of a sparrow

Hannah Duddy, Glasgow, Scotland

THE WORD

Equipped with special Rosetta stone
In a maze of abstract data
Instincts immune, the scrawling drone
Aloof from rhyming dogma
His gifted mind, dormant prone
Behold. The scholar, grapple stanza

Literal verses in metered sonnet
Skillfully written in sculptured way
With coded message and rhyming couplet
Avoiding pronoun and clever cliché
Free speech. An ideal not to allay
Politeral correctness, still to let sway

Lateral literature espousing form
Dated works no longer the norm
Latter day troubadours embracing rhyme
Imagine the scene, *Passage of thyme*
Freestyle the first choice to deliver cheer
The word, now fashioned for contemporary ear

Tom Guild, Cowdenbeath, Scotland

TO A SOLDIER IN THE TRENCHES

I can feel the blood trickling down your muddied face
Swollen feet drenched in rain-soaked slime
Poppies do not dance in the black encrusted fields
Only blood red rivers flow over years, through time

I can feel your lungs choke with mustard gas
Lips cracked and sore
Like splintered ice on a skating pond
The guns at the front a deafening roar

I can feel your head burst with the cries of men
Blocking your ears with a frostbitten hand
Soldiers beside you tumble into gaping graves
Arterial blood sprays like golden grains of sand

I can feel the chest pain
Suffocation, a lost fight
Dusk brings a sky spangled with twinkling stars
A half moon heralds a cold winter's night

I can feel your pain as you plummet from life
A sad release from suffering and war's din
Snow gently flutters, a blanket for your soul
I claim to feel your destiny but I can only imagine

Jacqueline Bain, Paisley, Scotland

PITS

From the platform of the leather shop upstairs
There's a bird's eye view of the tanners' pits,
Vast dye vats, ochre, saffron, madder, murex, indigo,
Manned by rheumatic, bare-legged refugees
From the Middle Ages. And from our Bourj viewpoint
We look out over the medina's suqs and alleyways,
A thick, black pall of smoke from burning olive pits
Rising above the drab ceramics works. Squatting inside
Around the walls, a group of sullen, bearded men chip out
Mosaic tiles, the size of thumbnails and avoid our eyes

Norman Bissett, Edinburgh, Scotland

LETTER FROM NH

On the envelope, your crow writing
spells an address
where I no longer live.

that I loved you once
seems almost as bland as
what to cook the kids for dinner.

Small, blue sheets
where your words wrestle to fit;
the folds (worked easy like the hinge of our knees)
mark the months we were apart,
(the other women).

That I belonged elsewhere once
shocks me.
My daughter yells questions up the stairs.

Emma Strang, Laurieston, Scotland

221

AUTUMN

Morning fog, freezing and damp
A grey shroud covering the land
Spiders webs like white lace doileys
Suspended in hedgerows
The mid-day sun disperses the gloom
Embracing with its warmth

In the park, children scuffle through dead leaves
And knock down chestnuts
Their dog yelping with excitement

At dusk, an icy wind springs up
Tearing leaves from branches
And whirling them in a mad caper
Russet coloured, brown and yellow green
Carpet the ground

Bereft of foliage and silhouetted against the horizon
The trees have a stark beauty
Overhead, a skein of geese straggle across the sky
Their weird honking cries attracting attention
Their flight an indicator

A Harding, Perth, Scotland

LOVE

Love saved me
Love shown to me by others, others who did not know me
But suffered the same affliction

The power of their love rescued me, rescued me
From the death path I was beating for myself

Love almost destroyed me
The love my husband had for me

For it was a selfish love
He loved himself better than me

Theresa Bradley Baxter, Motherwell, Scotland

TOTAL CARE

On supermarket shelves among ten dozen
One is not alone. The orange bottle
Comes with promise. She compares with ease
The shine and volume. Brilliant, vibrant, soft

And no more compromises, she can have it
All right now for two pounds ninety eight
The label says and she believes. A precious
Moment pops the vision in the hopeful

Trolley of her perfect life that smells
Of mandarin and elderflower bargains.
There's no mirror to remind her of

Her short and alien stubbles, aerials.
She spends a lot of time in front of shampoo
Bottles combing hair that is no longer there.

Britta Benson, Condorrat, Scotland

PRETTY COLOURS

Sitting on the bathroom floor
A small box room with a cold blue flowing through its
paper-thin walls
My hand gripping orange-yellow onto the rough, dark green
carpet.
I reach up to the light string and I pull black.
I sit in evil darkness, the room disappears, gets sucked into
this power.
Burning red, freezing desolate grey
All these feelings, building up inside me
I can feel the anger, dark green, maroon, flowing
Like a rapid river through my veins
This brutal golden moment.
I feel a dirty red now
Dark, sorrowful blues swirling and joining with the blinding
yellow in my mind.
They were believing her, everything she said
Purple-black lies, I knew that, but they didn't.
I sat, pastel blue, see-through, drip, dropping from my
eyes.
Everything was *my fault*
The lime green of not knowing what to do.
I felt a blue seeping through a roasting maroon anger.

Nula Glenn, Dykehead, Scotland

MOONLIGHT ON THE MERSE

It was as if the heavens had gently kissed
The peaceful earth and the sky's sweet dreams
Had showered the sleeping world
With the petalled light of shining blossoms

The air drifted through the fields
Of surge swelling ears of grain
Gently rustling the waiting woods
Under the radiant eyes of nocturnal stars

And my soaring soul
Its wings outstretched
Flew through the pastoral peace
As if returning home

Arthur Parsons, Coldstream, Scotland

SUMMER SONNET

The world was edgy on that afternoon;
the sun biked down, the landscape fizzed in haze,
a bee might buzz but dogs and people lazed
or quarrelled on that blistering day in June.
In Sicily, Mount Etna groaned and spat,
forests in Spain were licked by fiery tongues,
the merest stir was balm to air-strapped lungs.

Here I was, beached upon a dampening mat,
my hermit thoughts cracked up as pigmy pods
when drops of water splashed upon my head.
You look as if you need a drink, he said.
I peered to see him, haloed like a god.

It's weird the wizardry that love can spin,
the world backed out, and I saw only him.

Muriel Ferrier, Dundee, Scotland

AS I WAS GOING TO ST IVES

As I was going to St Ives, I met a man with seven wives
Every wife, she looked so fine, oh how I wished they could
be mine

And every wife had seven bangles
Slung about her curves and angles
Every bangle, seven sapphires
(Set in silver so it transpires)

Every sapphire caught the light
With seven facets, clean and bright
Seven servants followed, laden
With bag and case for every maiden

Yet though his fortune fair had swooped
He stood quite bowed, thwarted and stooped
Though stood a man with wives so fine
On his forehead, seven lines

Though no more than twenty five
This lucky man, with seven wives
Seemed an old man - torn and haggard
As along the road he staggered

As I was going to St Ives, in his plan I saw the flaw
For when a man has seven wives, he has seven
mothers-in-law

Lucia Crossan, Glasgow, Scotland

226

MY CHOSEN LAND

This is my adopted land
The place I choose to live
Hoping people understand
I still have much to give

I need no oath of allegiance
To bind me to this land
The faith that guides my conscience
The flag by which I stand

I'm part of Scotland come what may
I'll shout it from on high
I'm part of her I'm proud to say
I'll love her till I die

Ann Odger, Linwood, Scotland

MY FATHER

Your first gift to me was life
Unsought but gladly given
You hoped a boy, an heir
Name carrier, with features fair
No contrast ever was more clear
Tow-headed, amber-eyed
Opposite in all, including gender
Yet welcome never was more tender

Time passed. Roles were reversed
The child is father of the man, they say
Speech, sight, control all slipped away
Impotent watching is perverse
Such suffering so bravely borne
Release him God, and let me mourn

Grace Tweddle, Crieff, Scotland

227

DYSLEXIA - A WILDERNESS

My head, my thoughts, a wilderness
Letters jump randomly from the book
Instructions circle in disorder
Numbers and lists laugh and mock
People chanting stupid, stupid girl

A teacher's red ink slashed across the page
A smack on the leg in reading class
A childhood blighted
A lifetime of frustration
A life enacted as a stupid, stupid girl

Letters stick in senseless words
Instructions grind slowly to a halt
Numbers and lists in disarray
All caught up in a stagnant smog
The thick grey mass of a stupid, stupid girl

The fog lifts, a curtain drawn
Words, instructions, numbers settle
Soothed into order and understanding
A city of clarity evolved in hell
I am no longer that stupid, stupid girl

Dina Nicoll, Selkirk, Scotland

Welcome to the Short Story Society

Even if you have never had any prose published before, you should submit something to the Short Story Society. It's the perfect platform for your writing talents and gives you a fantastic opportunity to get your work published. Our aim is to help writers to create short stories and get them published and appreciated.
There's no membership fee to join the Society. To be a member you must submit a short story. If we do accept it, we will publish it in a compilation of short stories by other authors and give you five copies of the book.
We will also put your story on our website at shortstorysociety.co.uk for visitors to read and enjoy - in the months leading up to the publication of the finished book.
"Having a short story published is a wonderful and inspirational learning process for all authors - especially those who have never had their prose published before," said Peter Quinn, Managing Director of United Press, publishers to the society.

Your next step is to submit a short story. It could be handwritten or it could be typewritten. It could be on email or any kind of disc. You should send it to:
The Short Story Society
Admail 3735
London EC1B 1JB
www.shortstorysociety.co.uk
email - info@shortstorysociety.co.uk
phone - 0870 240 6190
fax - 0870 240 6191

Your story can be on any subject. It can be aimed at children, it can be a ghost story, it can be a love story, a horror story, a true life story.

£1,000 to the winner

All top poets never miss sending an annual entry for the National Poetry Anthology. Even if you have won through previously, and had your poetry published in it, this free competition is always open to you. And as it's the only big free poetry competition of its kind, it's the first one you should put on your list to submit your work to.

It's the biggest free annual poetry competition in the UK. Around 250 winners are selected every year, each one representing a different UK town. All winners are published in the National Poetry Anthology and all receive a free copy of the book. Many of these poets have never been published before. Send up to THREE poems (on any subject) up to 20 lines and 160 words each, by the annual closing date of **June 30th** to -

United Press Ltd
Admail 3735, London
EC1B 1JB
Tel 0870 240 6190
www.unitedpress.co.uk

One overall winner also receives a cheque for £1,000 and the National Poetry Champion Trophy.

Another £1,000 to be won

A poem about someone or something from your home town can win you a top prize in this annual competition. Anyone can submit up to three poems for the competition. The top poem will win £1,000 cash. There is no age limit and no entry fee. "The poem can be about something or someone from the poet's home area," explained United Press Publications Director, Peter Quinn. "It can be descriptive, historic, romantic, political, or personal - anything you like, as long as there is some local connection.This competition is open to anyone and is completely free to enter - so what have you got to lose?"

Send up to THREE poems, up to 20 lines and 160 words each, by the annual closing date of **December 31st** to the above address.